# WHAT'S NEXT

## AN EXPANDED 21ST CENTURY TIME STATUE HARVEST

**Robert F. Morgan**

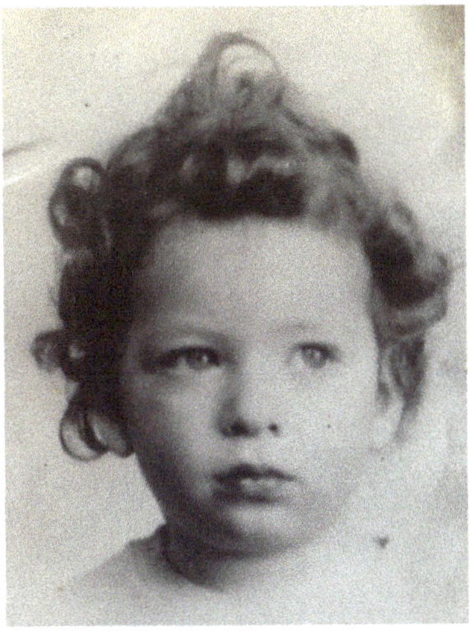

ISBN: 978-1-885679-38-3 paperback



Morgan Foundation Publishers. Email:
**morganfoundation@earthlink.net**

Web page:
**htpp://www.morganfoundationpublishers.com**

# WHAT'S NEXT

## AN EXPANDED 21$^{ST}$ CENTURY TIME STATUE HARVEST

Robert F. Morgan

# BREAKING

**BREAKING NEWS: On Day One, far in advance of the holiday, the President's executive order forced all opposition state Turkey Ranches to deport their millions of undocumented Turkeys back to their Home Country.**

**Turkey's President Erdogan Speechless.**

# CONTENTS

# Dedication

**Theme:** *Here Comes the Sun* George Harrison

According to DNA analysis, about 160,000 years ago there was a mother in East Africa who had many children. There were other families living there and then.

Yet it was her children that survived to spread through the earth. Through the millennia, to become the human family of today.

Shaped in appearance by different surroundings, shaped in action by diversity in culture and its gifts.

The 21st century opportunity is to bring all these cultural gifts together, home. The Olympics begin this for athletics. Much more is possible.

On a much smaller scale, this book harvests some of our best glowing 21$^{st}$ century time statues along with many new ones.

Our East African mother's descendants are all our cousins.

They reside now in our temporal geography.

What follows is written for them.

# Time Statue Harvest: 21st Century

**Themes:** *We are Family* Sister Sledge; *Reunion* Bobbie Gentry; *Sing Our Own Song* Buffy Sainte-Marie; *The Good, the Bad, and the Ugly* Danish National Symphony Orchestra; *Walk on the Wild Side instrumental* Jimmy Smith; *Time Will Tell (theme from The Wizards)* Susan Anton.

This book in the *Time Statue* series is a 21st century harvest from a lifetime of special events. Time is a place. Each moment is a statue in time, always rooted in that time and that place. In this book's lifespan revisits to international time statues from the first quarter of the 21st century, they are followed by ones in the rest of the century that might come after. Or not.

At this writing, the 21st century is but a quarter spent. Still, these are highly interesting times to inhabit. Events now will determine whether children born today will in fact be able to experience their full life through the rest of the century. The challenge for survival is ours.

Still, these are highly interesting times to inhabit. Events now will determine whether children born today will in fact be able to experience their full life through the rest of the century. The challenge for survival is ours.

Best maybe to share a look at experiences reflecting the times we inhabit.

These were often recovered in dreams. Some in sleep, reliably every 90 minutes, some in that semi-wakeful twilight time between waking and getting up, some while day-dreaming apart from whatever reality surrounds.

The ones to follow here are time statues, those more interesting that glow in recent memory, while actually living on in their current temporal geography.

*She was the matriarch of a large family. Lived in an isolated region, inside a mountain top. When each of her children became an adult, they began the SEARCH. Gone for a year, off in a new direction, unknown territory. Most survived to come home when the year was up. To share what they had learned, what or who they brought back. These gifts were absorbed in the family, celebrated as due, for a restful year at home. Then, as the next year began, off again in a new direction. Searching for new treasures. Thanks to this SEARCH, they flourished. Not sure if they ever knew that they were living, on a much smaller scale, the best harvest of Earth cultures. One our entire human family was approaching.*

DNA scientists discovered that all humans alive today can be traced to a mother about 160,000 years ago in East Africa. She lived near other human or humanoid families at the time. Yet over the eons, setting aside trace DNA of Neanderthal or other unique contributions, it was her children alone through their generations that survived, and thrived, to inhabit today's Earth.

As our human family.

Yes, across the Earth, we are all cousins.

Over this epic time, it is estimated that those born in one place died no farther than five miles away. Yet in 160,000 years they did eventually inhabit the planet.

Even if we assume that about half of all these people each millennium died before reproducing. Died from various disasters from predators, climate, eruptions, flood, fires, and, of course, each other.

Isolated in pockets of the earth, survivor skills evolved into culture. Psychologist Art McDonald described best how their local environment shaped them. Eight hundred years in snow country and the skin was white. Eight hundred years in hot jungle required nocturnal living and the skin was black. In this way surviving enclaves developed through natural selection the best protective skin- red, gold, brown, black, white. McDonald brings in the weather, available food, epidemic resistance and much more. Where each colony lived, their surroundings remade them.

And their culture. Language, weapons, creations, traditions, art, music, ideas, insights, technologies, ways of living together, ways of living with the land. Progress forward.

In each of these separate cultures there were true gifts and some grave errors. What was missing was some way for each cultural pocket to connect with the others.

Now, in our modern century, we have seen transportation advances connect them, all over the globe. Meaning the DNA was mixing to more diverse and adaptive forms.

And then, we have seen a communication revolution, connecting us even more thoroughly. These both opened the doors to a powerful sharing of the gifts from every culture. The Olympics every few years, based only on athletics, is a beginning and a model for much more.

And, careful now, some cultural byproducts are not gifts. Including seeds of destruction- nuclear war, epidemics, monopolistic greed engendering an accelerating climate change on a path to a planet devoid of life.

Still, we now have the means to harvest the *best* of each cultural pocket, true fruits of 160,000 years of planetary dispersal. Bring them all home. We can do it *now*.

Gather in this harvest while time still allows it.

# Introduction

**Book Theme:** *Time Will Tell* Susan Anton from the movie *Wizards*

***Time is a place. Each moment is a statue in time, always rooted in that time and that place.***

> *When I was five years old, my mother always told me that happiness was the key to life. When I went to school, they asked me what I wanted to be when I grew up. I wrote down 'happy.' They told me I didn't understand the assignment, and I told them they didn't understand life."*
>
> –John Lennon

> *"Because we are born for a brief span of life, and because this spell of time that has been given to us rushes so swiftly and rapidly that with very few exceptions life ceases for the rest of us just when we are getting ready for it. It is not that we have a short time to live, but that we waste a lot of it. Our lifetime extends amply if you manage it properly."*
>
> –Seneca, 65BCE, 2004 AD

Time is a place. Each moment is a statue in time, always rooted in that time and that place. Memory allows us to visit them.

After eight decades of this, I have amassed a library of memories. Stacks after stacks of time statues archives.

So much that it can take minutes or more to access just one memory and only with patience. Elders do better at this when we imagine our search as an ordering at a restaurant. Then, usually, it will come.

Arriving late? But it will come.

From the viewpoint of age, we can view these memories in their entirety as a grand tapestry. Not necessarily arranged in order, chronologically.

What is a good guiding strategy for navigating these patterns, this treasure in an elder's experience? Maybe it's ones that were meaningful or fun. Sometimes both? Usually based on real past experience. Sometimes not.

All of these can be shared.

**Now:** Well, at least some statues in time can be worth a visit. Or, on reflection, a revisit.

*"Peter Rabbit"* was a children's play I took my daughters to when they were very young. Peter began each day with great joy for the inevitable adventure. A day for him seemed like a whole season for us humans.

Remember in our own childhood how the beginning of the summer vacation seemed like the opening of endless days? For the shorter lifespan rabbit, each day was like that. It was a revelation for me. A fresh approach.

Learning to perceive the *Umwelt* (world view) of animals has the added benefit of enhancing empathy for own species.

For one, humans have great individual variations of time perception. Working with older people, I often saw anxiety about how few years of life it seemed that they had left.

I had been working with the full spectrum of human aging and life extension experts, Jim Birren to Timothy Leary. They approached the subject with biology as cause and with psychology as consequence.

What if we reversed the order? What if seniors with the life expectancy of less than a decade approached each day as a season in itself? Instead of ten birthdays and out, why not 3,650 individual seasons to savor, one at a time?

To do this, the senior would need to slow the rocketing passage of time engendered by similar days. Magnified by retirement or illness, one day is much like another. They go by in a flash.

This may be comforting but life then goes by quickly. But if each day was differentiated as its own adventure, time will slow down. Life extension occurs experientially. For some, those who accomplished this, they said it helped very much.

We're not rabbits. We live much longer.

Or so we can learn to experience that longer more fully.

Can each of our days and the moments within them become simply statues of adventure in time?

Although many are protected by metaphorical police tape. Worth the trip?

Building on the five book series "*Time Statues Revisited*" and the follow-up "*Future Time Statues*", once again we come to Einstein and Vonnegut: the temporal community is a place. Each day we finish is fixed for all time. Or is it? We can revisit, this time for new and more challenging ones.

This time we go to the even more interesting ones, in two newer *Time Statue Harvest* books. This 21st century one follows the 20th century one.

To help, each chapter begins with a link to a musical theme.

As we get older and remember our past, our regrets are more often what we did *not* do than what we did.

Either way, a revisit to worthwhile remote events in this century seems worth the return trip.

Despite some statues best forgotten.

To navigate effectively in our own normal environment, it is entirely reasonable to consider time as linear and irreversible.

A nonlinear approach will naturally unearth exceptions. The passage through time carries us forward, evolving and adapting.

In our nonlinear world, if we are open to it, we can find ways to detour against the current as part of our healthy development.

It makes for a richer tapestry than had been expected.

Each moment we live includes our action as our art. Good art or bad art, all that we do sculpts a second-by-second statue to inhabit that time and that place.

The artist continues to live in the limited moments of this lifespan community.

Yet the consequences of this art can travel ever further, transcending dangers and obstacles, to shape a better future for our human community.

In this way, we can too.

-

**Note:** For this 21st century focus, this last book in the *Time Statues* series has print enlarged. Many of us who have reached this century, after living through much or most of the 20th one, appreciate print sentences that are easier on the eyes. I do recognize that the younger readers are more likely to be reading this as the electronic version. There on their phone or laptop, they can control the word size. Some of us still prefer the old school option of an actual hard copy book. Helpful in propping doors open, killing invading insects, or as backdrops for zoom calls. Every generation has its own approach.

Today all generations face the same 21st century existential challenges. We can work together to inhabit the future. When we do, we succeed.

Lots of paths to choose from.

Consider carefully.

# Optional Music Themes

**Theme:** *Put another Nickel in* Teresa Brewer

Just below the chapter title is listed an optional theme, music or video. Some of readers may prefer to listen to this before, during, or after the reading of each chapter.

If before, you can play it soundlessly in your mind while reading. You enjoy reading as a kind of movie experience with music enhancing the experience. This feature is for you.

Other readers may find this a distraction. Or they may just want to avoid any online interference to their reading. These readers may have grown up in the early or even pre-television generations where radio stories dominated.

That required imagination to supply the picture and any music. For them, we recommend skipping the optional themes entirely.

This omission is for them.

# The Discovery of Poison Ivy

**Theme:** *Poison Ivy* Coasters

***"Two roads diverged in a wood and I—***
***I took the one less traveled by,***
***and that has made all the difference."***
**-Robert Frost**

# 2000s

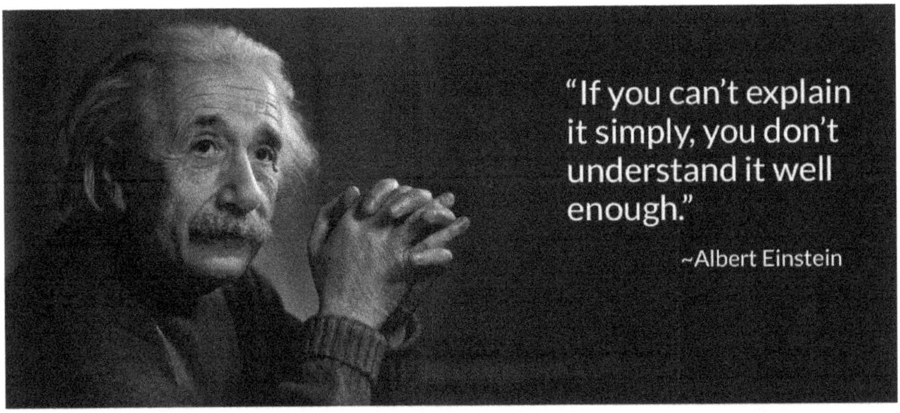
"If you can't explain it simply, you don't understand it well enough."
~Albert Einstein

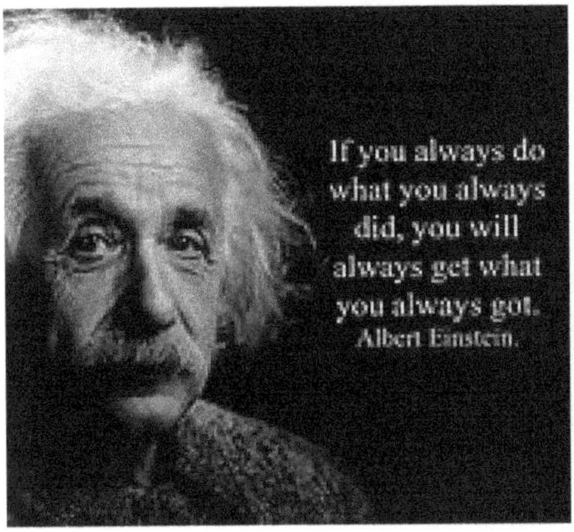
If you always do what you always did, you will always get what you always got.
Albert Einstein.

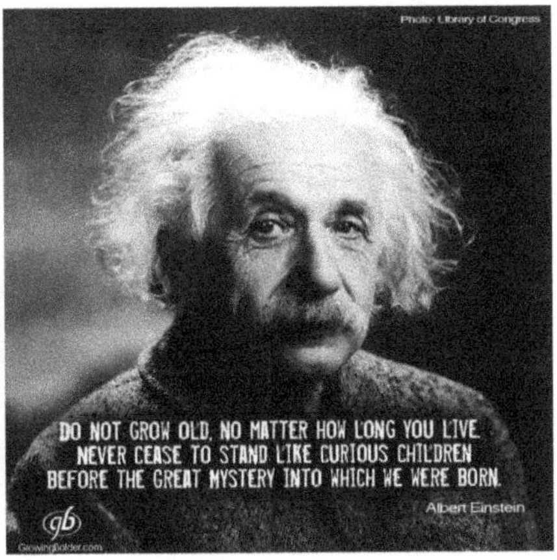
Photo: Library of Congress
DO NOT GROW OLD, NO MATTER HOW LONG YOU LIVE.
NEVER CEASE TO STAND LIKE CURIOUS CHILDREN
BEFORE THE GREAT MYSTERY INTO WHICH WE WERE BORN.
Albert Einstein

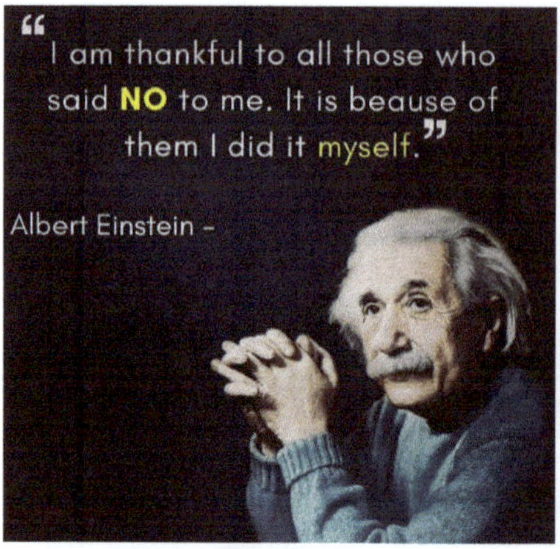
"I am thankful to all those who said NO to me. It is beause of them I did it myself."
Albert Einstein -

ALBERT EINSTEIN
STAY AWAY FROM NEGATIVE PEOPLE. THEY HAVE A PROBLEM FOR EVERY SOLUTION.

Question everything

**Including this:**

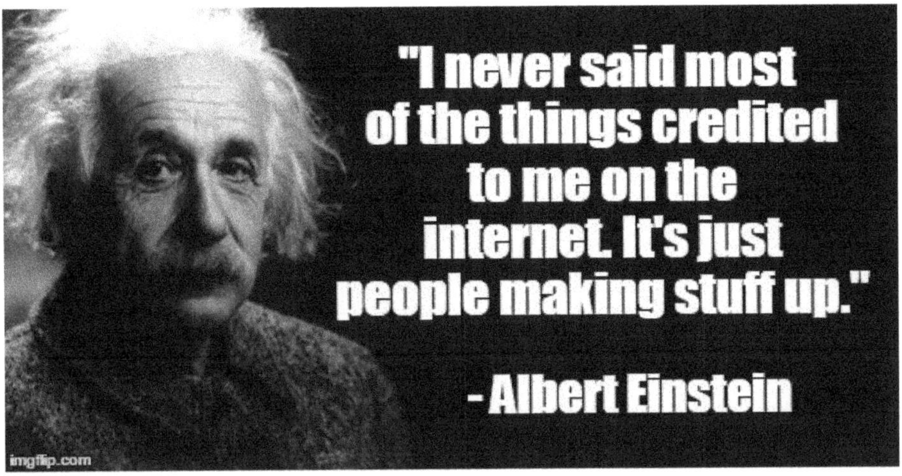

# The Day of the Hobbit

**Themes:** *Run Through the Jungle* Credence Clearwater Survival; *The Sorcerer's Apprentice* P.A. Dukas/London Symphony Orchestra, or in Disney's *Fantasia*.

Found in Guam's jungle is the Monitor Lizard.

While it does have a venomous bite, its main defense is bacterial infection. Crawling with lethal disease, the indigenous Chamorros warn their children to stay as far away from them as possible.

The bacterial defense has also been a major cause of the disappearance of human populations. Historically, Europeans in the middle ages believed that deadly pneumonia or plague was brought on by bathing. Royalty typically were bathed only twice in their life, at birth and at death. Hence the heavy use of perfume. This of course brought on epidemics of disease. The Black Plague of medieval times wiped out a third of the population. Survivors had immunity and continued to carry lethal bacteria from the unbathed lifestyle. This was a defense as strong as the Monitor Lizard had. The indigenous peoples of North America had little or no protection against the bacteria crawling on unwashed European pioneers. The majority died.

Whole civilizations, per archeological digs, seemed to disappear in a generation. Where did they go?

Epidemics may well be the cause. Epidemics from contact with people or animals carrying disease for which they had no protection.

Was this another reason for the Great Wall of China? Defense against foreign plague?

Going much farther back in time, what happened to the Neanderthal? Where did they go?

They had lived for eons in Europe before our branch of the human family made it out of Africa to settle in their territory.

The fact that modern people of European descent usually show Neanderthal DNA of one or two per cent gives evidence that the contact was often close and intimate.

The Covid-19 pandemic has sensitized us to the historic role that a lethal virus and bacteria may well have played in our erratic patterns of survival.

Science today has noted that the Covid-19 plague turned out to be even more dangerous for those with traces of Neanderthal DNA.

Where did the Neanderthal go? Into the ground apparently. And into our DNA.

Our human family has branches that may have been and continue to be as dangerous as the Monitor Lizards are in the jungles of Guam.

## Enter the Hobbit

It was May of the year 2000 in Guam, entrance to the 21st century and a new millennium.

Somewhere in that month I passed out on the stairs on my way to teach my class.

I was only out for a minute or two, fast getting up, saying I was fine, pretending that I was.

After my class, the Dean wanted to see me. He said that sometimes people like me, walking to the university on a hot day like that day, well, they just fainted. But I knew that wasn't the problem. I never faint. Maybe I needed a checkup for my heart. Soon.

Still, the next afternoon I set out again for the walk to my campus. I wore heavy shoes and asked my feet to stand tall, to not let me pass out. I could feel "*trouble be knocking at my door*" as some Pacific islanders like to say. Want to resist, keep that door locked.

I got about halfway to campus when I saw her. She was barefoot yet walked out of the jungle with ease.

Nobody walked in the jungle barefoot, the snakes alone … and there she was.

She looked like a child with an older person's face. She was about three and a half feet tall. She wore a yellow dress and had a yellow ribbon in her hair.

She calmly started walking next to me. Said "*What would you like to know*?"

Years after I still think of all the questions I should have asked.

At the time though, we were approaching that usually vicious and massive dog chained to a pillar, a chain keeping it just short of the road. It always tried to bite anybody passing, more like wanting to tear somebody apart, not a great part of my daily walk.

But today! When I walked by the dog it quietly watched me, not even rising. Still wasn't friendly. but smiled the way dogs can smile, mixed both hateful and happy it seemed.

I asked the girl "*Why is that dog usually so full of rage? From being chained up?*"

She regarded the dog a second. Said "*No. She had only one litter and it was drowned in a sack. She has wanted to kill people ever since. Chaining her up is necessary and she knows it.*"

I asked a second question: "*Why is she so quiet then with me today?*"

"*She can sense your heart is stopping and starting. She knows you are dying. It makes her happy.*"

We walked quietly for a bit while I digested that.

I objected "*I wasn't the one who drowned her puppies. Why so hateful with me?*"

Yellow dress shook her head. "*She sees all humans, your kind, as the same. Being around humans for so long changed her. Humans are like that too you know.*"

We got to a shelter, a bus stop with plastic seats and a narrow roof.

It was beginning to rain. Windy horizontal Pacific rain, intense, but short.

Tourists asking about the weather in Guam are a joke. It's always raining somewhere on the island and the sun is always shining everywhere else.

To the Chamorro of Guam, there are usually only two locations on earth: Guam, and then everywhere else on earth is "*off-island*". Not counting the locations lost in time: "*Take the east road and turn past where the post office used to be.*"

We waited. When the rain stopped, not a long wait, we continued on our way.

Clearly, she did not seem used to such a lack of questions. She stopped as the jungle on our left came to its end and the campus began.

She smiled and said "*Well, what do you have for me today?*"

I used to carry edibles for children but that day I had nothing. I shrugged and said "*Nothing today. Maybe another day.*"

She looked stunned, as though nobody had ever said that to her before. She then turned and walked back into the jungle.

I got a little closer to work, opposite a high school playing field, before I passed out.

I woke on the ground not long after. Noticed my left ankle was broken at a right angle to the leg. Shoe had been trying to do its job. I reached down and snapped the foot back into place at the ankle.

When I woke again, the paramedics were there. The high school student that had called them was saying "*When his leg snapped, the crack sounded like a rifle or an explosion. So loud!*"

Apparently my heart block was expected to be fatal and soon. So they called the only cardiologist on the island (excluding the military base which was off limits).

There had been two cardiologists but this one was at the funeral of the other.

He got there just in time to put in a pacemaker, a more current model replaced it eventually but I still use one now 21 years later.

That was my first pacemaker and it had been the last one on the island. Saved my life.

A year later, veteran of two open heart surgeries, I was well enough to be back in class.

Being in a wheelchair then, my class was held inside my leased hotel apartment, in the long living room with a semi-circle of six tables and chairs.

Since the hotel was only at the edge of the campus, students were pleased to come there.

Not only was it better than the usual classroom but my hotel had covered parking, great for the episodic rain torrents.

The first thing my students wanted was a complete update.

So I told them about the girl in the yellow dress with the yellow bow in her hair. They called her a "*Taotaomona*".

They said "*You should have given her a gift!*"

**Note**: Not long ago, they found evidence in Indonesia of an ancient separate branch of humanity, termed "*the Hobbit*". This is a label that annoys the diminutive Indonesians on the island they found the Hobbit skeleton.

Here is a better description of what they found: "*Homo floresiensis ("Flores Man"; nicknamed "Hobbit") is a small species of archaic human which inhabited the island of Flores, Indonesia until the arrival of modern humans about 50,000 years ago. The remains of an individual who would have stood about 1.1 m (3 ft. 7 in) in height were discovered in 2003 at Liang Bua on the island of Flores in Indonesia.*" Phys.Org, Feb 2016.**https://phys.org/news/2016-02-mystery-hobbits-humans.html**

More recent news articles include a photograph of a surprised anthropologists realizing that this branch of humanity still lived in Indonesia.

Maybe a lesser surprise if they had looked more closely at their own photos in the news. To realize that some very small smiling local people shared their picture.

Stories of the "little people" abound in cultures around the world.

Menehunes in Hawaii, Leprecauns in Ireland, Yunwi Tsunsdi for the Cherokee, Tautaumona in Guam, and the surrounding islands.

Are they still around, this alternate branch of humanity? Well, Pygmies still live in Africa.

Was the person walking with me that day, a 'hobbit'?

Staff at the Smithsonian, reconstructed a face from the skull they found in Indonesia.

Here it is.

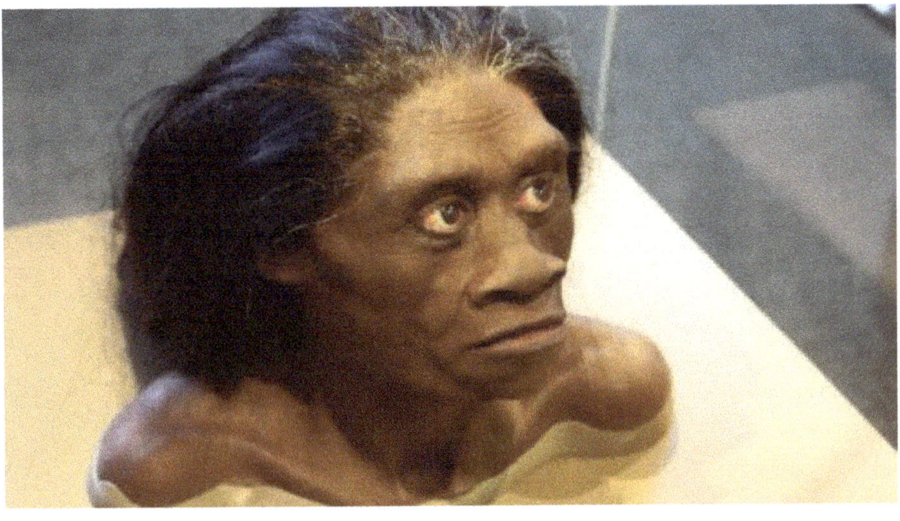

Yes. Add a yellow bow. That's her.

# Exit to Stanford

**Theme**: *Money Honey* Elvis Presley

Later in the year 2000.

Once the *Enter the Hobbit* events ended in Guam, my health insurance gave me two destinations for cardiac surgery care: The Straub Heart Hospital in Hawaii or the Stanford Hospital in California.

Straub was 3,000 miles closer so I went there first.

## Straub

The open heart surgery seemed fine. Only later was I able to learn I had fallen off the mini-size operating table during the operation.

I had liked and trusted the surgeon so I definitely paid attention when before surgery he had explained the key after care rule- "Keep your arms against your side for 24 hours once you wake up in intensive care. You will have had your chest sawed in half vertically so we could reach the heart. Stretch your arms and the chest incision may not have adequately healed, so it could split open on its own."

I woke up in the intensive care unit or ICU. I was intubated so I could not speak. A nurse came up to do a brief body scrub and pulled on my right arm to do so. I shook my head no and kept it against my side. She saw this as bad behavior and tried to pull the arm away. I wouldn't let that happen. My arm stayed against my side. The nurse got another nurse to help and they each took hold of an arm. Pulled. I was weak from the surgery but this was survival. My arms stayed by my side as they needed to be. The nurse enlisted two more of her brethren and now a pair of nurses were on each of my arms pulling as hard as they could. I wasn't budging. The original nurse spent a key moment swearing at me, maybe too long a day? She then brought in a doctor to drug me into compliance. Who instead chewed them out for risking my post-op life. After that it was war.

I still couldn't speak. I was groaning in pain for two days, groaning being mocked by the nurses to my wired up face. Finally my surgeon came by and saw that the nurses had never given me the painkillers he had prescribed. He put them in and my pain got reduced. Nurses chewed out again.

Time overdue for me to get rid of the throat intubation that blocked my ability to speak up for myself. I gestured that I wanted the throat block out and the surgeon, shrugging, sent the order out to make this happen. The technician showed up that Sunday in his church-going suit, briefly listened to the nurses, and, scowling walked over to me to remove the intubation piece. He put his foot on my chest, shoe and all, and yanked the unit out of my throat.

To his surprise, my respiration jumped to 100 % and my chest held together. Relieved, I thanked him with my first words in days. Curses sure. Bless his church-going heart.

The final hurdle to discharge was the debate between my surgeon and the neurologist. My surgeon had wanted to put in my heart a tissue valve. My neurologist wanted to put in a mechanical valve.

Being my body, I was the decider and had chosen the guy with the knife.

The neurologist may have been hoping to move enough mechanical heart valves for a company-paid vacation. In any case, his many third gear pacemaker racing drills nearly burst my already tired heart.

## Guam

I survived, returned with my bovine tissue valve and pacemaker to home in Guam. Stayed in long term care for a while.

Stacked in with patients. One dying from final stage liver damage from chronic alcoholism, happily drinking the wine his family smuggled in. A sex worker in a low cut dress moving through the male patients, not washing up between customers. No thanks.

Only one MD on the roster but he was the owner and I never saw him there. Oh, and one male nurse, friendly, selling probiotic pills for upset stomachs by the bottle to patients. That would save my life.

Straub's final gift to me was a hospital infection identified as MRSA. Said then and there to be incurable. Home at last, out of Long Term Care, my chest bones began to dissolve.

Local doctors tried to halt this challenge with six weeks of daily home-administered Cipro Antibiotic. Met some great nurses. But no success.

This time I took the insurance choice to travel to California.

## Stanford Hospital, Palo Alto

It was Christmas when I got admitted. Beautiful grounds and buildings for a billion dollar healing center, among the foremost in the world. My modest Guam insurance got me in.

On the way to my room, an intern told me the paintings on the hallway walls were rare and renowned. I couldn't tell because each of them was wrapped up like a Christmas present, complete with ribbon bow.

At the doorway, I could see that, possibly due to my modest financial status, I would have a roommate. He was already there. Buzz cut hair, stocky, looked to be at least 400 pounds. He was surrounded by nursing staff. The nurse settling me in my own bed said he had been constipated for two weeks and now, finally he was getting a successful enema. A special event I was there in time to appreciate.

My roomie was not particularly friendly. Post enema, he only sent me a few nods and growls. Then turned on a football game on the TV facing our beds. At that point I couldn't focus my eyes on television so I just listened. Football viewed as only sound sounded like deadly combat. The occasional crunch and a player carried off on a stretcher, each time with a snorted laugh from my roommate.

The next day my tests were complete. The following morning was surgery.

They did the open heart buzz-saw chest option again. Debrided my MRSA invested deteriorating bones, scraping off the invaders as much as they could see. It took hours.

My favorite doctor of the bunch, a Dr. Chang, told me later about the debate. A few staff felt I was too far gone to commit so much time. But Chang prevailed. Feeling better than on arrival, I was sent home to Guam.

But not long after arrival, the bone deterioration started up again. My main doctor there had run out of ideas so my case was reassigned to his intern, thereby protecting his patient survival record. As to his record, he hoped to regain his former government post in another year. To be employed by the government, you may not have been convicted of a felony *within the five years prior to that employment.* Only one more law-abiding year to be clean, legal.

So no progress there. Then I remembered that male nurse selling Garden-of-Life probiotics. For digestion.

But it occurred to me that all the antibiotics, too overwhelmed by MRSA, were still effective in destroying the good bacteria my immune system depended on.

Without these internal soldiers, the invading infection was multiplying, colonizing on my chest bones, feeding on the great calcium thereupon. Until much of the bones on my right side were diminished or missing.

So bringing in the probiotic bacteria platoons might recreate the immune system.

Feed on the invaders. Find homes safe inside my grateful body. Well. Worth a try.

Binged on the probiotic pills daily for 10 days. I did feel somewhat better, so maybe ...

I was scheduled to return to Stanford before I could find out if it worked.

## Stanford Hospital Again

I kept the flight to go back to Stanford Hospital. Dr. James Chang had the second debriding marathon all scheduled. Tests on arrival. Prepped for surgery.

Dr. Chang arrives first thing in that operation morning. He carried some papers, x-rays, and was pulling a little girl in a wagon behind him. They both were smiling, happy. It was Sunday and he always spent it with his daughter.

He asked me if I knew the opening line of the Hippocratic Oath that medical doctors took. I did: "*First of all, do no harm.*"

He said "*Well, there you go. Why would we go ahead and do this operation when our tests find conclusively that MRSA is entirely gone from your bones? Maybe you can tell me what you did for this miracle? After the last operation we thought you were way too far gone to ever return. Anyway, we are sending you home.*"

His daughter, now on his shoulders, impressed by his tone, sent me a great smile.

I smiled back and thanked her.

I went home. Missing a few bones but MRSA never came back.

I published, told friends, after surgery please take strong probiotics. Decades later, probiotics are now standard in better hospitals after an intense antibiotic series. Also decades later, I emailed Jim Chang to see how he was doing, considering another surgery there for something else. How was his sweet wagon-riding daughter?

*"Oh. She finished medical school. She's a doctor now. No wagon."*

Stanford had its issues as do any hospital. Most staff though are well paid, highly effective, and pleased to be working there.

And its opulent funding was normally matched by equally wealthy patients. Consequently, when I was rushing to leave, to make my plane on time, I was being helped with the two male nurses that had been with me for that whole stay.

They had just realized I didn't have my own plane chartered.

Used to very wealth patients apparently. This for them was a surprise.

One said in disbelief "*You're not flying COMMERCIAL!*"

Economy all the way home.

# Definition

**Theme:** *Baby Elephant Walk* Henry Mancini

*In the black and white movies of the first half of the 20th century, a key word beginning many sentences was "Evidently" or based on evidence. You could identify the era just by the use of this word. A new generation's substitution for the rest of the century, reflected in movies, was "Apparently" or based on what we see. The 21st century's generations kept apparently for a while but then TV and online sentences just began with the word "So" based on a pause to think. In time, twitting, texting, and their progeny went for the leanest quick communications, based on speed without need or time to think. "Critical thinking" could still be found though increasingly that first word eclipsed the second. So, the following, evidently and apparently, came to mind.*

It was a quiet afternoon in Palo Alto. The 21st century was new. More than a dozen faculty of the past Institute of Transpersonal Psychology were gathered around a conference table. To perform the episodic ritual of sharing the multifaceted personal definitions of the discipline they taught.

This time Arthur Hastings began. He had developed a complete set of components that formed the skeleton of our academic program. Impressive and we all were familiar with this perspective. Next was Bob Frager, the past founding president of ITP and still a key faculty presence. Bob had made Arthur's physical component come alive with the essential training addition of Aikido and other martial arts. But his definition was much wider. Bob saw Transpersonal Psychology as the *whole* of psychology, a more comprehensive view of the discipline that included the components our students studied along with all else psychologists were supposed to know. Next came Charles Tart.

Charlie focused the definition on a single word: "*spirituality*". Perspective diversity for sure but each faculty member with their own definitional validity.

My turn next. I had published a chapter on Transpersonal Psychology in my 1980s books on life extension and the measurement of human aging. I chose "*Human Potentials*" as a definition then. Something my 21st century students preferred as it encapsulated their motivation for being at ITP. Before I shared my own differential perspective, I told a story.

"*You all likely know the story of the blind monks defining an elephant by each touching a different part of his anatomy. The led to a very diverse set of definitions depending on which part of the elephant they had digitally explored, each one correct in its own way for that pachyderm portion.*

*Or so it would have been had not the elephant been in a very bad mood that day.*

*The funerals for the blind monks were exquisite and touching (so to speak)."*

I conceded that I had added my own ending to the story, logical as it seemed to me (remembering an elephant in Thailand that had tensed muscles in suppressed rage as I touched it, over not getting any peanuts I think, and weeks later killing some tourists in a rampage).

Each definition had been right, mine too, and our elephant was fine with all of our descriptions. It does require a lot of them.

And peanuts.

# Prelude

**Theme**: *Go Your Own Way* Fleetwood Mac

My first precognitive client.

Being the only psychologist in this half of the remote mountain county was like being a country doctor. I got the full range. Way beyond my learned or experienced competence, Well nobody else was there for them. So I had to learn fast. Continuously.

She was in her mid-twenties, tinted glasses, intent. Said she was worried about her mental health. Why? That took a while. But eventually: *"I get music in my head and write original songs. I keep them. Show them to nobody. Just creating them is enough. Makes me happy. Then, in a few years I hear my very own music on the radio. But somebody else gets the credit. Time after time. Am I crazy?"*

I said let's start there. After some tests, I shared that her reality contact was fine, her intelligence well above average. So no evidence of crazy. What was it then?

It could have been a factitious disorder. That is, she was making it all up. Why? Checking out the new doctor?

Attention? Interesting word "*factitious*". Describes our era well. Commercials in a constant flurry. The best being exaggerations, the worst scams or propaganda. Always I wonder '*what's the catch*?'

Prescription drugs marketed on TV or online directly to the consumer- at least, by law, they list side effects. Damage risks at times include "*death*" and then show happy people buying the product. (What if *anything i*nfluential people said would be immediately followed by side effect risks or other sad consequences? What a great political campaign that would be!) Factitious?

And yet, I believed her. She was serious in her assertion that her music was being claimed by others. In fact, she said, since she wasn't crazy, what about others taking her songs? And wasn't it weird about her that she did the same music first? That's why she was afraid to tell anybody else until now.

So why was this happening?

Delusional or valid? I decided to follow the valid option. Tackle the 'why?'

*"Well, there are a few reasonable explanations for this. The first is something called 'parallel evolution' in biology. That's when two entirely separate species of animals or plants develop in exactly the same way. It can happen with human experience too."*

She questioned: *"To you?"*

*"Sure. Whenever I come up with an original idea, I write it down. Then I do the best search I can to see who already thought of it before I did. Usually there's somebody to thank or cite even though they never helped me. They just got there first."*

*"Well, in my case, I was the one that was first."*

*"And they don't know it. So maybe you might consider copyrighting or otherwise insuring credit for your music when you create it."*

*"Well, what if THEY are the creators and their music just comes to me before they create it? Cause it seems to flow into me without any work on my part."*

*"You're very honest. So: Hard to thank them for something they haven't done yet?"*

She's smiling now. Finally having a long suppressed conversation. Relaxed. Wants to know more. I do so. But kindly left out quantum connections at impossible distances.

*"You could be experiencing 'precognition'. Receiving from the future before it happens in the present. Time is a place. We can remember the past, some even learn from it, but parapsychologists think that at times, special people may actually get visons from the future. If this is what's going*

*on with you because of your musical ability, see it as a talent."*

Now she's happy. "*So I can tell everybody about it!*"

*"Maybe not. Just in safe settings like this or with people you are sure you can trust. Some psychiatrists, not understanding what we have discussed, may be frightened, may diagnose it as a problem and try to 'cure' it. Could be trouble knocking on your door, a pretty risky problem."*

*"Okay. I'll be careful. So thanks for all this. By the way, you should try receiving songs yourself. You might be surprised."*

By the check-in a month later she was doing fine. Happy.

I suggested she might consider offering her talent to Broadway songwriters, thereby saving them time since their own work, or your prior originality, could be anticipated.

She laughed.

No, all she wanted from her visits with me was to know she wasn't crazy or brain damaged. Now she could see it as a talent, she had no need to make it pay.

Well, she added, maybe a trip to Las Vegas someday to bet on music futures.

# Lucy Two Feathers

**Theme:** *Lucy in the Sky with Diamonds* The Beatles

Lucy glowed.

My daughters did this.

And then, long after they were grown and gone, here was another child, about six years old, lighting up her world. Creative, fearless, friendly, genius smart, mature for her age, intense, deeply hurt.

The hurt?

Her parents were divorced. She lived now with her mother in a duplex located in remote northern California. Far from her past friends. She had no brothers or sisters. She missed her father every day. They had been close. He was an angry man apparently. Killed himself while Lucy had not been long in that duplex.

She loved her mother too. Luckily it was reciprocal.

Summer was beautiful there.

With my wife Becky, we had moved into the other side of the duplex.

Lucy's mom gave us a quick tour. Same layout as ours. Lucy slept in the upstairs bedroom, mom downstairs.

I saw Lucy that first day sitting by herself near where the other children were playing.

I said hello, introduced myself as her new duplex neighbor, asked why she was sitting alone. She smiled and said *"They're okay. Just kind of still babies. Big as me, same age, but kind of crazy. I'll take care of them if I can but .."*

*"Not really friends. I felt like that too at your age."*

*"You did?"*

*"Sure. Grownups were too big, too old to be the friend I wanted. Except for a fewe and that made the difference."*

*"You were lucky. Grownups don't like to be friends with me. Somehow. Maybe scared people won't understand.*

*Maybe laugh at them. If I had a grownup friend, I'd keep it secret."*

*"Well, we live in different halves of the same house. If you like, I could be your friend."*

*"My secret friend?"*

*"Sure."*

That night, after Becky was asleep, I heard a knock on the wall next to my side of the bed. I realized that it was Lucy on the other side. I knocked back. Heard her laugh.

The next morning her mother came by. Becky was at her job but it was me she wanted to talk to.

*"My daughter tells me, in great confidence, that you are her 'secret Dad'. I told her no, that you were a psychologist, and just being friendly. What's happening here?"*

I was fascinated that Lucy had changed 'secret friend' into 'secret Dad' but I suppose that was what she needed. Mom was reassured that I meant her daughter no harm, already was married and didn't need her to be a wife. We had a friendly conversation. She said she was lucky to share a duplex with a psychologist since her only child sure needed one. I suggested she get an outside psychologist too for what her daughter, and her, were going through.

I spent some great time with Lucy that summer. Gave her some of the Maurice Sendak *Where the Wild Things Are* little figurine toys to role play with.

After being reassured that they weren't really alive, she threw herself into it.

With imagination and insight she concocted wonderful stories. Some we steered into her own tragic family situation but always with happy resolution.

Lucy seemed happier then. Began spending time with the other children nearby.

Said she felt at first like a babysitter but decided to be a "psychologist" like me and look out for them, be their friend. Not a secret one though.

The wall knocks, short of Morse Code but nightly, continued. With my wife's kind understanding. They were brief and Lucy's mother said she needed to hear a return knock before she would go to sleep.

Summer was coming to a close. We would soon be moving out. Lucy sensed that things were about to change again.

She was picked up each weekend by her grandparents and wanted me to meet them maybe go with her on the visit. I declined the latter but agreed to meet them.

It didn't go well. They never got out of their truck to meet me. Just glared, then drove off with Lucy.

Her mother told me not to be concerned. She had told them that Lucy believed I was her "Secret Dad" and they were convinced that I was dangerous.

Nor did they know what a 'psychologist' was.

Nor, for that matter, did Lucy.

So Lucy took the grandparent turbulence in stride but did really want to know what I did for a living as a 'psychologist' or as me.

I gave her the long definition of what I do as a psychologist with no patronizing. No vocabulary simplification.

She listened carefully. Nodded. Said "*I get it. But what I REALLY want to know is what YOU do?*"

Oh. Deeper. A basic truth?

"*Well. I try to make the best wishes of good people come true.*"

She beamed at me. "*That's what I thought you did.*"

# Sharing

**Theme:** *Side by Side* Kay Starr

Sometimes this is called *"identification"*. Sometimes this is called *"empathy"*. Sometimes this is found in years of marriage. When couples finish each other's sentences, share the same dreams, begin to look more like each other.

What happens is that we become more like the people we spend the most time with.

Or even with animals. Ever notice how humans and dogs begin to resemble each other over time? Both body and mind, physical and behavioral. It has been noticed that domesticated wolves, our dogs, over generations of human contact take on human expressions never found in wolves. Of course, the humans living with these dogs may take on more than a few of the canine aspects.

If your spouse circles the bed three times before getting in, beware. Sniffing the butts of arriving visitors another warning sign. And what cat owners might do... Well, you get the idea.

The key is that this sharing goes in both directions.

I do remember a very early 1930 demonstration of this when a married couple of psychologists adopted a baby girl chimp named *Gua* who was close to the age of *Donald*, their own baby boy. The two were raised together for almost a year. The focus was primarily on Gua with Donald as a normal comparison. In their first months together, Gua outscored Donald on intelligence tests, falling behind only when the psychologist parents attributed Donald's speech abilities as an advantage. Gua's vocal cords didn't work effectively for that. Still, this was years before chimps were taught sign language (see the *Next of Kin* book).

All the focus on Gua's childhood in a human family eventually had a reciprocal impact on Donald, a human child raised with a chimp sister. When Donald began making chimp sounds, the parents exiled Gua to an animal facility. There she died a year later.

I could find no followup on Donald as an adult. Wonder who he married?

It was the beginning of the new millennium. I had just begun a faculty job at the Institute of Transpersonal Psychology in San Francisco. I was to meet with 30 new students in the clinical psychology doctoral program. They had already begun their field placements. As that class began, there were only 29 students. A few said the missing student was always late but she would be there.

I began by putting this identification reciprocity concept in context. I told them about the "*medical student's disease*" in which some always worried that whatever disease symptoms they were learning about also seemed to be in them. I asked them to pay attention in their field placements to see how they might be taking on the problems of their client, acting them out in their own life, unless they were vigilant.

About then the missing student arrived. She stomped into the classroom, scowling, and sitting down hard on a seat, arms crossed, glaring at me.

"*Something wrong?*" I asked.

"*Just takes me longer to get here from my field placement. I suppose you want to make a big deal about it?*"

"*Hmm. Who were the clients you were working with?*"

"*Teenage girls! So what?*"

She was surprised when everybody in the room laughed. This was going to be a great class.

-

## Source Note:

Fouts, R. and Mills, S.T. (1998) *Next of Kin: My Conversations with Chimpanzees*. New York: William Morrow. Kellogg. W. N. and Kellogg, L.A.(1933) *The Ape and The Child: A Comparative Study of the Environmental Influence Upon Early Behavior*. Hafner: New York/London.

# After the Seminar

**Theme:** *Stayin Alive* Bee Gees

It was a very hot southwestern state. So hot that my normally evening classes were beginning to look like the after sunset future of all education and commerce. As the planet's Anthropocene continuation made daytime increasingly intolerable.

My night seminars had a pattern. Limited to a dozen or so students (my record was 23 but it worked) with chairs rearranged in a semicircle facing my desk and the video screen. Everybody can see everybody else. The lighting is indirect, non-fluorescent, full spectrum, soft and safe. In front of each seat is a Ghirardelli dark chocolate in its wrapper. Next to the chocolate is a fresh cool bottle of Fiji water. All preparation for a three hour weekly class, with a half hour break after the first 90 minutes.

90 minutes of class is the attention limit for most students, even the advanced ones I see in these seminars (movie producers take note). As to those students, the night ones are usually the best one could hope for. They usually have day jobs, families, and other responsibilities. They are

mature with a deep interest in the subject we will cover. They are nurses, military, sales- working people.

We would meet for that one night every week for a full all-season semester. Using group protocol, introductions first, nobody left out, several rounds for greater depth, we by the second meeting knew each other pretty well.

This particular seminar's subject was the psychology of trauma. I alternate that with a lifespan class in other semesters. The students were close to finishing their doctorate, becoming colleagues.

One of them in our depth introductions shared, as best he could, that his wife was dying from cancer. That he might miss some classes if it got worse. Lots of group support descended upon him.

By the third meeting of the seminar, my concern about him had escalated. Sure, he was sad and stressed. But there was something else. He was angry. Suppressed rage. Suppressed and, it seemed, turned on himself.

A formula for suicide.

Not what you want in a future therapist. Or in another human- we are all cousins after all. So I asked him to stay a few minutes after class. He agreed.

"*How's your wife doing?*"

*"No change. All the preparations for her passing have been made. I give her all the companionship I can. She's very undemanding and gracious. I love her so much."*

*"How long has she been in this condition?"*

*"Ten months."*

*"Wow. What a long time for such stress. For both of you."*

*"It seems endless. But I'm holding up. If she can deal, I can too."*

*"Are you angry?*

*"Sure. She doesn't deserve this! Of course I'm angry."*

*"At yourself?"* Pause.

*"Yes. I wish I could make her healthy again."*

*"More. What part of your anger is hiding?"* Pause. Reflection.

*"I have monstrous thoughts, feelings. Sometimes I just want her to die and get it over with."* Tears.

*"Of course. You want to end the pain for both of you. Thoughts must be free as you know. Let yourself understand this as a way to cope. Then your actions can be more helpful. To you both. Any freeing of such fantasies will free you to live. Do you want to live? Do you choose life?"*

He did. And he would. By the next week's seminar his rage against himself was gone.

Sadness and resignation yes.

Though now he would live to help his eventual patients survive as well.

# 2010s

**Valentine** *From an attic in Northern Ireland* (*Or not*)

**Theme:** *Irish Blessing: May the Road Rise Up to Meet You (When Drunk Again)* Grex Vocalis

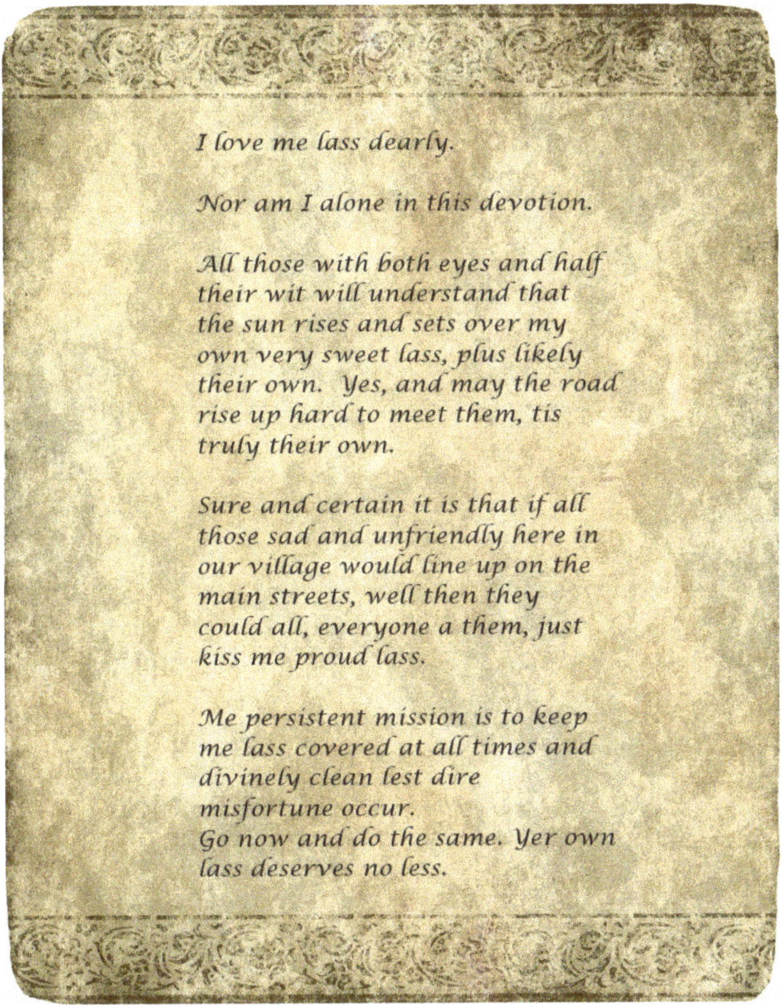

*I love me lass dearly.*

*Nor am I alone in this devotion.*

*All those with both eyes and half their wit will understand that the sun rises and sets over my own very sweet lass, plus likely their own. Yes, and may the road rise up hard to meet them, tis truly their own.*

*Sure and certain it is that if all those sad and unfriendly here in our village would line up on the main streets, well then they could all, everyone a them, just kiss me proud lass.*

*Me persistent mission is to keep me lass covered at all times and divinely clean lest dire misfortune occur.*
*Go now and do the same. Yer own lass deserves no less.*



**RF Morgan  Artwork by Mikael David Owl**

# The Night Principal

**Themes:** *After Midnight* JJ Cale/Eric Clapton; *Graveyard Train* Credence Clearwater Revival

*It was 2010 in Singapore, not that long ago. I was a visiting professor at an Australian University located there. The guard at the entrance and I had both once been staff sergeants, each in the military of our own country. Soon we were good friends. One day, as I was leaving, he pointed to a bird at the top of a large tree. "Did you know that here in Singapore we have the best talking birds in the world?" I did not. So far the bird songs I had noticed had only two notes and no lyrics. Apparently this simple male competitive mating music still was enough to attract female birds of their species. He waved at the special bird on the tree to get its attention and said "Hello! I have an American friend here." The bird replied: "Hello! Food?" Much to the point. "Sing first," said the guard. The bird obliged with the standard two note song. I responded by whistling a little of the song "Stairway to Heaven." When I finished, the bird silently contemplated me for a few seconds. Finally it said "Go Away!"*

That was at the Australian university in Singapore. The CEO had been an elementary school inspector back in his own country (spying on the teachers to keep them compliant?) and now was beyond his depth in running higher education for gifted adult students.

He became an insomniac, seemingly doing all he could to reshape the university campus to be the elementary school he had once been comfortable in. This included his leasing a campus in Singapore. A former elementary school.

That seemed to have been a very good deal. Good space, solid two story construction. It had been on the market for quite some time, so it was inexpensive. There was a reason.

Chinese culture shuns talk of death lest it bring that very thing upon the speaker. Even in San Francisco, buying a house there mandated full disclosure by the seller if anybody had died in that house. My Singaporean Chinese clinical psychology students had some struggle to learn grief counseling therefore but powered through it.

The elementary school that had once thrived upon the campus was built around a very dedicated and charismatic principal. He set generations of young children on successful life paths, He was much loved.

So much so that when he died, the elementary school died with him. Before closing it completely, the principal was buried in its courtyard. His wishes were to lie where his beloved children had once played. Undisturbed, a memorial.

It worked for a long time. Singaporean businesses, eager for expansion in the small space the city-state provided, still had nobody wanting to build offices over that principal's burial site. Yet in time it had to be on the market.

Until the Australian inspector built his campus addition on top of it.

This CEO mandated elementary school hours. Even the professors were supposed to be there at daybreak and leave before dark. Life near the equator had consistent day light times, all one season all year. So this campus hummed during the day but closed down completely once the day ended.

Except for me that one day.

I was through with all the regular work by 3 PM.

I walked the long red carpet arrowing past all the first floor offices toward my office at the end by the Clinic. Just in front of the finance office there was a rise in the path, not much, but enough so the Malaysian Finance Officer warned me to avoid tripping on it. I hadn't noticed it before and now asked him about it.

He had me step into his office. There he explained why the CEO had paid so little for this campus lease. The swelling in the carpet was above where the elementary school principal had been buried. All staff had been instructed to ignore this by the CEO so nothing was done about it, mild tripping hazard or not. The first floor offices had been built over the courtyard playground, and the grave, with the CEO forbidding local superstition to delay his bargain.

I wondered out loud if this was just a story to prank visiting professors- both of us. The Finance Officer said no, but urged me not to discuss it with anybody else. The CEO was emphatic about this, had fired a few staff just for mentioning it. His own fear? Or concern about alienating his student financial base?

I finally made it to my office.

Eager to finish the first draft of my textbook *Trauma Psychology in Context.*

My writing style in those days was to stick with a project until it was done, no matter how long. In those healthier years of my 60s and 70s, I could tolerate working around the clock without a break. Tolerate? It was great fun.

Sure I had a heart problem with a pacemaker saving my life back at the close of the 20th century. There in Guam I had been legally dead for a while. Changed my view of the world, of life and death. An amazing experience, another story. But soon after I regained my health, I got in shape. Found joy in writing. Here years later in Singapore this was to be one of those days.

I barely noticed when all the other people on campus had left, doors locked, lights out. I was so close to finishing everything. I only stopped to call my wife and tell her why I would be home late. She understood.

Midnight. The light in my office was the only light on in the university campus. I could see the book draft almost done now. Time to add photos, references, edit. Maybe another hour or two.

An old Chinese man stood in my office doorway.

I don't recall how he was dressed except that it was unremarkable. He seemed agitated, annoyed. Pointed at the wall clock. Clearly he thought I didn't belong there at that hour.

Let me know with gestures that I was to leave.

I supposed he was a night watchman. Not speaking out loud because he didn't speak English? Strange since all employees were mandated by the CEO to only speak English at this Australian outpost.

I gestured at the work on my computer and nodded at the clock, asking by signing for a little more time, almost done.

He shook his head no, still clearly put upon. Then turned and moved back into the dark building. He had made it clear that I didn't belong there at that time of night.

Though I felt he had reluctantly given me time to close and leave.

One AM. I was almost done now. Just finishing touches. Loved how the book draft had shaped up. He was back.

This time with clear gestures to leave immediately. Pointing to the wall clock again.

I nodded, held up ten fingers for the pick-up time I thought I needed. Then he was gone again. I supposed he wanted me out of there before his shift was over, before daylight came.

Three AM. Fully done now. Got the twelve hours I had needed. Longer by two hours than anticipated as usual. But done! As I closed up the office, lights there flickered and went out. Footsteps approaching from the dark.

I had a flashlight and followed it outside through a side gate of the locked down campus to the street and walked home. Very happy with the book project completely done.

Concerned that I had upset the watchman. Tired, finally tired.

The next day at work I asked around to see if the watchman had complained. If he was okay. He was, after all, just doing his job.

Always the same response: "*What watchman*?" And "*The CEO would never pay somebody to watch a dark and empty building*"

I wished the old man, the Night Principal, peace.

Never disturbed his evening again.

# Bite Me

**Themes:** *Flight of the Bumble Bee* Rimsky-Korsakov, Katica Illényi; *Honeycomb* Jimmie Rodgers; *Snake Farm* Ray Wylie Hubbard

Angelina Jolie, for World Bee Day, promoted her conservation effort to save the diminishing bee population and consequent risk to the world's food supply by a photograph in *National Geographic* showing her covered with (friendly) bees.

Women in many countries shared this photographic way to show love for bees.

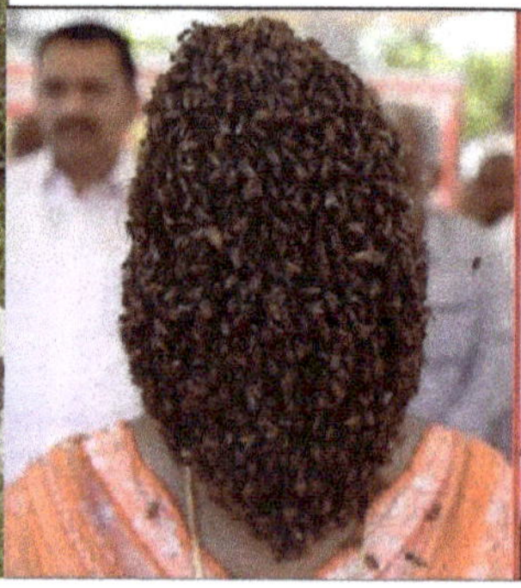

Some in their very own way.

Inspired by this, the Rhune Corporation chose a fresh and innovative advertising campaign for its new edible skin exfoliant "*Bite Me*". A beautiful woman runs from something in the woods. She is scantily dressed and in heavy makeup, much as you would expect to see there. Then she stops only long enough to quickly apply a jar of *Bite Me* all over her body. Suddenly she is covered with happy butterflies and blends into the woods.

This can be tried at the Butterfly enclosure in Albuquerque's *BioPark*.

Or many other places where butterflies or their distant insect cousins may be found.

Even in remote locations, woods or jungle for example. And that is what happened next.

A global fad emerged where beautiful women attracted butterflies with the *Rhune* new skin care exfoliant *Bite Me*.

Of course, sometimes the product attracted the baby butterflies, the caterpillars:

The CW

But the publicity always helped sell the product.

Butterflies and caterpillars were not the only woodland creatures attracted to the product.

For those, hoping to lure photogenic little creatures, surprises abounded.

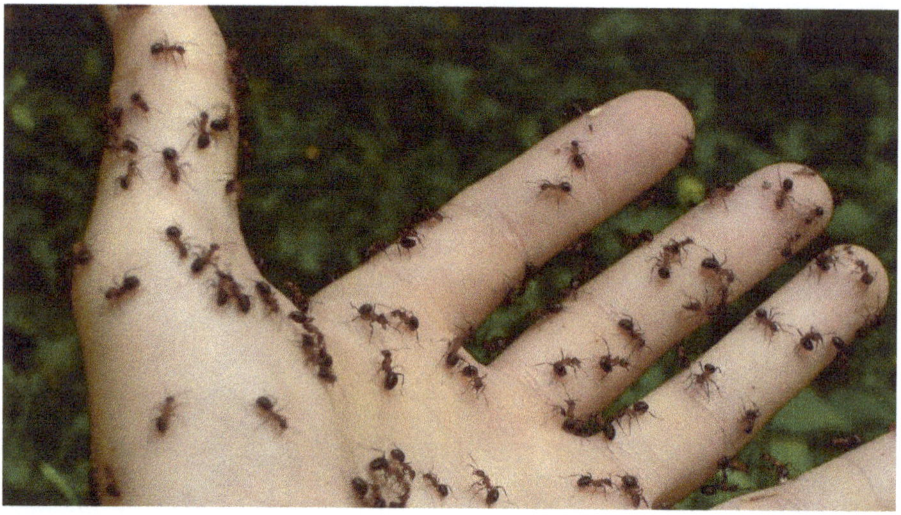

Often this international fad for *Bite Me* took place in risky locales. This just added to the attraction.

If dangerous enough, it did at least attract professional photographers or TV cameras.

Or their cell phones.

*Bite Me* sold very well and its company was delighted.

Some got too carried away. Literally.

Eventually other animals much larger than butterflies and far more dangerous, hungry, were attracted to the product as applied.

Never underestimate the intelligence of large predators.

Did the exfoliant name *Bite Me* encourage them?

Of course, "bite me" can be a reciprocal concept.

From the beginning.

Caterpillars might not be limited in size.

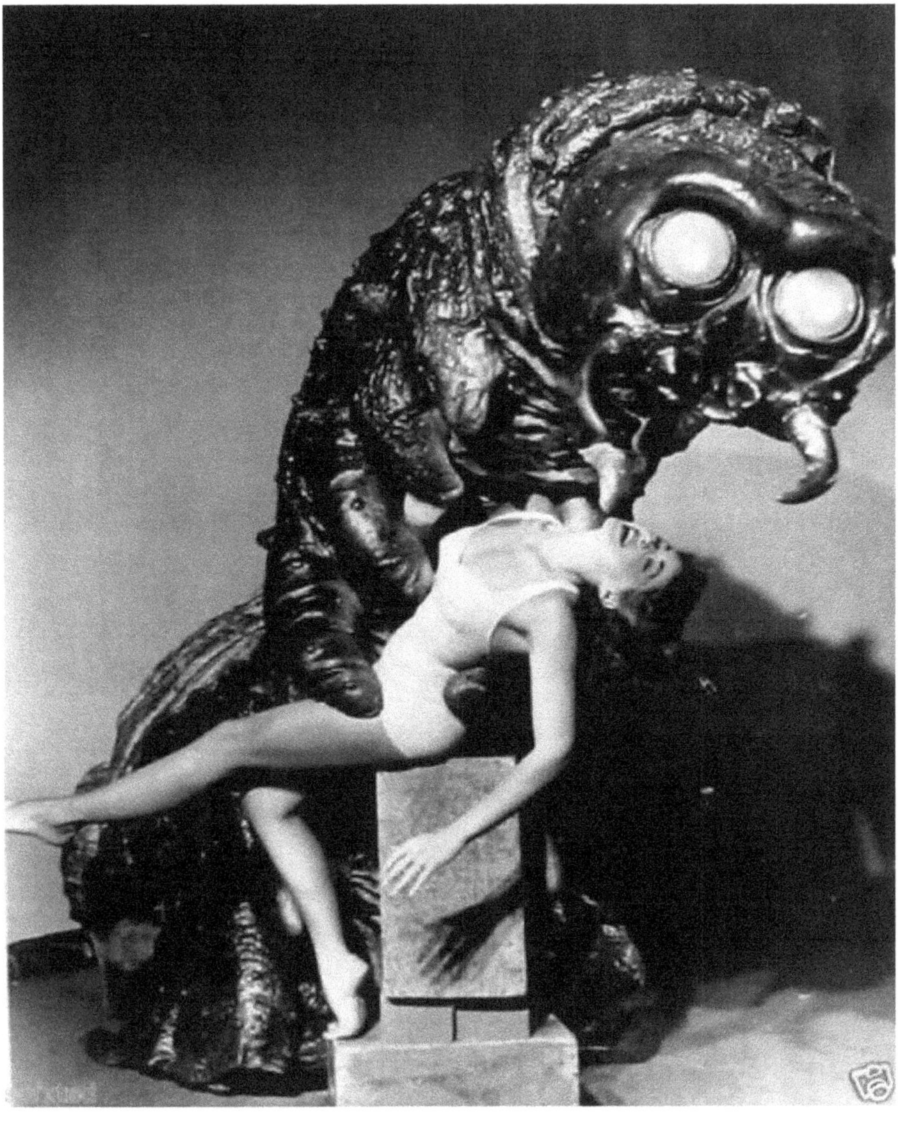

Although even that could sell the product:

That suggested a solution, a new path to encourage.

When a monster is attracted to the *Bite Me* exfoliant, love the beast.

Conquer the tiger to make it your friend.

This is the Senoi method for reframing nightmares (A.K. Morgan, 2011, 2018).

Look at all the times we have enjoyed seeing this work out well before.

Theme enters here: *I Feel Like Singing, So In Love* Dan Hicks

Dreamwork done well can improve reality profoundly.

To work directly on improving reality is much more of a challenge.

So, following the conservation example of Angelina Jolie, the *Rhune* company encouraged their customers to love *whatever* was attracted to them,

But only when their *Bite Me* exfoliant was used.

Many succeeded.

We will always think well too of those who tried the exfoliant and did not survive.

**Note:** Bees like flowers. Be generous.

# A Letter to Charles Tart

**Themes:** *Mystery Train* Elvis Presley; *I Still Believe* Tim Cappello; *Riders on the Storm instrumental* The Doors

*European science, followed by most North American academics, demands that any unusual event must be explained by some tested explanation before it can be taken seriously. Some outlier scientists are just fine to explore the unknown without knowing the why. Empirical first, they are Inductive and not Deductive- they explore at the outset from the experiential facts. The true scientific prelude. Being in that number, I have had some of my own experiences that awakened my interest.*

*As I once wrote to Charles Tart in this letter:*

## Brushes with Experiential:

*Hello Compadre- I finally got around to reading your 2009 book "The End of Materialism", which of course is more about escaping the limitations of what is called materialism, since materialism is still with us. Maybe what was meant is more like leaving the city limits, the place where it ends for others. The city still remains, but the wide world(s) beyond hold much more to explore for those still curious.*

*To do this, you gather evidence and anecdote, expressed in the good natured clarity of Charles Tart.*

*In any case, I very much enjoyed the book so live with it, my friend, this is a fan letter.*

*It brought to mind a few passing memories of my own consistent with the anomalous ones that you explore consistently, at least one of these being an important one engendered by a chapter in your first famous book from a half century ago.*

*<u>San Francisco 1973:</u> The Camel Races were being held at Bay Meadows Race Track. I took Dianne and her girlfriend Vicki since none of us had ever seen camels race. Nor would we that day. Camels only were in the first race but they turned out to be indifferent to human expectation. Few if any ever reached the finish line. It was funny and fun though. Now, having seen camels meander, we were ready for the regularly scheduled horse races, another first for us. Dianne handed me the day's listing where the names of all horses were listed. She challenged me to pick the winner of race number one. It wasn't a friendly challenge. Dianne was very skeptical of the parapsychology explorations my students and I were doing by hypnosis at psychology's first professional school in its earliest years. I really wanted to meet this challenge somehow, so I studied the racing sheet very intensely, wondering what to say. I noticed what seemed to be a glow around one horse's name. I confidently*

*said the name out loud and suggested they bet on it. Dianne laughed and declined to bet. The horse came in first. Now both women were excited about my apparent ability to pick a winner. I was challenged to do the same for the second race. I suppressed my own surprise and with seeming confidence reached for the racing sheet. The desire to show off was strong in me. But this time there was no glow to be seen. Just a faint discoloration around one of the names. Hoping for the best, I chose that horse to win. They ran to invest all the funds they had with them on this horse. To my relief, that horse came in first. Now both Dianne and Vicki were true believers. They had visions of buying us a mansion, their own complete new wardrobes, maybe a cruise around the world. What was the Riviera like that time of year? I calmly accepted the racing sheet for a third try. This time I could see no glow or discoloration of any kind. Whatever ability I had experienced before was not to be found now. As had been my expectation. I tried to tell them this but they were having none of it. An exchange of that era was "Whatever happened to your get up and go?" with the answer: "It got up and went." Following this thought, I yawned, stretched, and said I was going home. Which I did. The indignation of my two companions lasted for as long as I knew them.*

*<u>St. Bonaventure University (SBU), Olean New York 1967-1969:</u> The low self-fulfilling prophecy or resistance to anomalous experience was called "psi missing" by*

*Gertrude Schmeidler. (I note she died the year your book came out but infer no causation in either direction.) I didn't like her "psi-missing" term as it seemed more like "psi negative" to me, an example of self-programmed failure. I did love her experiments though and set out to replicate them with the huge audiences beginning faculty, like me at that time, get in their mandatory introductory classes. Out of hundreds of students sitting in the auditorium, it was not hard to find a few volunteers who either believed telepathy impossible or actual. Most were agnostics on this point or at least too inhibited to take any stand. A coin was tossed by me 20 times out of the sight of all students in the class. The believers that volunteered in my classes never scored beyond chance level. The fervent disbelievers often (the majority of them) scored well beyond chance: with all or almost all guesses wrong. This made sense to me. We are much better at sabotaging ourselves to meet low expectations than guaranteeing success at meeting high expectations. Key football players betting on their own team may just be expressing confidence but if they are already playing at their best, then no enhanced performance can be guaranteed. Yet if those key football players bet against their team, then the probability of impaired success is highly likely. It is just easier to fail. Best to keep expectations high, even against all odds. (At one for-profit university owned by Goldman-Sachs, I advised the under-resourced faculty to think of their glass as 10% full).*

*This I replicated in class after class for two years at SBU, two years next in Nova Scotia at Acadia University, and four years finally at San Francisco State University. But 1975 was the last time I did this. For one, I had moved up the ladder to small graduate seminars and no more abundant supplies of non-psychology students. But there was another more personal reason.*

*My father had very firm opinions. He was absolutely certain that my interest in parapsychology was a waste of time. So at a family gathering I challenged him to participate in a Schmeidler coin tossing experiment. You see where this is going. As my children watched, their grandpa guessed every coin toss wrong. As he turned around to learn his score, he noticed the amazement on their faces and, I think, for a second he allowed himself some pride at thinking he got them all right. The results of course were announced as the opposite. Not only did he miss every guess, but, this failure, as he saw it, was being used to disprove his previously stated emphatic belief. He was not convinced that this demonstrated strong ability on his part, even if he used this ability against himself. Let's just say he wasn't particularly happy. I regretted embarrassing him that way. From that point on, I realized that most students seen in class, disproving their own disbelief by outstanding failure, would be made to feel miserable. There might be a few who understood this revealing of unexpected ability as an opportunity to revise their understanding of themselves and the universe they inhabit. Such people are hard to find in a population of skeptics usually impervious to divergent information.*

*Wolfville, Nova Scotia 1969: At Michigan State University five years before, Paul Bakan and I explored fast ways of sensory deprivation to experience hallucinations without drugs. The three key elements were lying down, restricted vision (papered over swim goggles), and restricted head movement. Within an hour, sometimes in minutes, people experienced visions not in voluntary control (something Arthur Hastings explored years later in another setting with his Psychomanteum research).*

*In a western Nova Scotia university I set up a lab to continue this work. One student who participated wanted to see if she could use our apparatus to see playing cards that I held while her vision was restricted. I agreed. I went through an entire deck of cards one at a time. Each time she visualized a card and reported what she was seeing. Often she excused herself because she was anxious about her performance. When we were done, I had the sad task of telling her that she had not been correct about a single card. Which met her catastrophic expectation squarely. Yet I noticed that she had picked the color of the card, red or black, correctly every time, something highly unlikely due to chance.*

*A few years later in San Francisco, where the 1960s were still alive and well throughout the 1970s, I noticed my daughters' primary school friends liked to play a card game where the winner was the one who wound up with all the cards. In each round a child had to guess the card every other player was holding, one at a time. The guessing got better and better over the summer, an actual learning curve. No experiment here, just children playing a game. Improving with practice.*

*San Francisco 1971-1975:* *The California School of Professional Psychology was our first American professional school, originally with just two campuses in San Francisco and Los Angeles. The first generation of students were generally as experienced (and as old) as the faculty. These pioneering students included Frances Vaughn, Benjamin Tong, Nathan Hare, Reiko True, Leonard Elkind, and many others eventually well known to psychology. They lacked only the doctorate. Without a core curriculum, we 13 founding faculty had the opportunity to fit the classroom training to the actual needs and interests of these very capable students. There would be dissertations with freedom as to focus and the innovation of a proposal that would be binding on the school once the proposal was approved. With such a free hand we generated innovative curriculum. Founding faculty member Andrew Curry, MSW, an African-American world-class expert on group process, created a liberal arts cluster. This included the Tantric Feets Dance Ensemble, the Freedom from Disabling Pathology Gazette, growth groups including psychodrama, alternative healing techniques, martial arts, even a course labeled Psychic Intuition. This last course offering troubled the school president, Nicholas Cummings, but Andy told him it was a philosophical discourse on "ways of knowing". Nick was already troubled with the San Francisco campus and what he called its 'curriculum buffet". He also wondered why mail from the Los Angeles campus was delivered to his San Francisco office in a day, while our San Francisco campus took a week to get to the same office. (This time distortion turned out to be a turning back of the postage meter so late submissions still seemed to have been mailed within their deadline.) Some of the innovations were brilliant successes and some fell flat. Possibly the best decision I made as Dean at the time was to bring hypnosis into the curriculum for the first year students. Eric Greenleaf did a visualization class and David Cheek did a gratis hypnosis training workshop. The students applied this learning very effectively to reduce test anxiety, enhance speed reading comprehension, and even pursue personal experiments in parapsychology.*

*Many of these innovations last to this day in very traditional graduate schools of psychology. Some of the more specialized additions given to first year graduate students carried on in uniquely progressive programs like the Institute of Transpersonal Psychology where Robert Frager built Aikido and other martial arts into the required curriculum. The early hypnosis training is still a goal I would like to see programs provide to their students as a core course.*

*Virginia 1979: I had read Robert Monroe's book while still working in Southern Colorado 1975-1978. I knew somebody who was working with maximum security patients, including the rapists and serial killers locked up there. I had already convinced the administration to stop providing weekend passes to town for these dangerous patients as behavioral incentives. In all fairness, I suggested to staff that those patients likely to be locked up for the rest of their life there without passes, might benefit by learning out-of-body experience so as to at least journey out of their imprisoned body. Obviously I hadn't thought it through. I was told they already did that all the time. Not a comforting thought.*

*Angel Kwan-Yin 1971-Today: Angel is my youngest daughter, born in Nova Scotia during our final days in Morgan House. Before she was a year old we had moved to a home in San Francisco, albeit with some challenge from US immigration. Although she was a newborn with blonde hair and blue eyes, her middle name convinced some bureaucratic cretin that we were trying to smuggle a Chinese baby in from Canada for sale in San Francisco. With substantial time and affidavits, we finally achieved dual citizenship and the right to keep her. The naturalization paper was stamped with her infant photo and baby footprint.*

*Angel as a toddler was called "Superbaby". She had immense strength. We might be sitting on a substantial living room chair or couch when suddenly it would start moving. A little giggle behind it would let us know that Angel was there. That continued up to about age two. One day I asked her to move my chair while I was sitting there to demonstrate her powers to some guests. She declined: "Little girls aren't strong enough to move big chairs with people in them" she explained, as an older boy had convinced her. I asked her to show us what she used to be able to do and she complied one more time. But that was the last. Psi negative again.*

*She did come when I, and even some other family or friends wanted her to join us, even if it was not out loud. She would come running down the stairs from her bedroom at any random time we did this, usually with a special welcome or other fun thing waiting. This lasted until age five. When some would say erroneously that her cognitive abilities would have just begun.*

*<u>Some last thoughts</u>*

*A small thing- you still refer to five basic senses in the book. From our colloquium discussion at ITP a decade ago, the basic ones acknowledged over the last five or six decades number 10. The five senses most think of are touch, taste, smell, sight, and hearing. This misses the next five which include the sense of hot and cold temperature (separate receptors as one can feel both heat and cold at the same time), pain, balance, and body position or kinesthesis. To be basic, each has its own specialized receptors and sensations. I learned this in Howard Bartley's class at Michigan State University in 1961, using his perception textbook. That leaves parapsychology pioneers not the 6th sense but the opportunity to find the 11th and on, many more than these basic ten.*

*Your definition of "spirituality" as different from religion is very sensible. On the other hand, the word allows hostile skeptics to conflate your perception of spirituality with the fraudulent spiritualists that Eric Weiss (Houdini) loved to expose or the Lillydale ones so embarrassing Elisabeth Kubler Ross in her senior days. (Or the Father Divine and other cults insisting that the death of their immortal leader was only a "dirt nap".) Ah well, a rose by any other name won't know the difference.*

*Whatever we label your journeys of understanding, your good-natured clarity in sharing them with us, this book and all that came before remain well worth reading. By now quite a few generations are the better for them. Much of this valuable information and insight is enhanced by the example of a scientist unafraid of genuine science. I appreciate even more having had an opportunity to work with you as a colleague and friend.*

*Robert Morgan, 2013*

# Rise of the Emoji

**Theme:** *Junk Food Junkie* (Larry Groce)

*Bill Maher warned us that the newer generations were so immersed in brevity that pairs of them completely celebrate Valentine's Day*  *by one texting the other with a love*  *emoji and the other responds with a "same" emoji*  .

Emojis have proliferated massively for the texting generations, a pictorial pandemic.

So much so that many began to see any photo as an emoji rather than itself.

Like these potentially new emojis:

Insight

Restraint

Respect

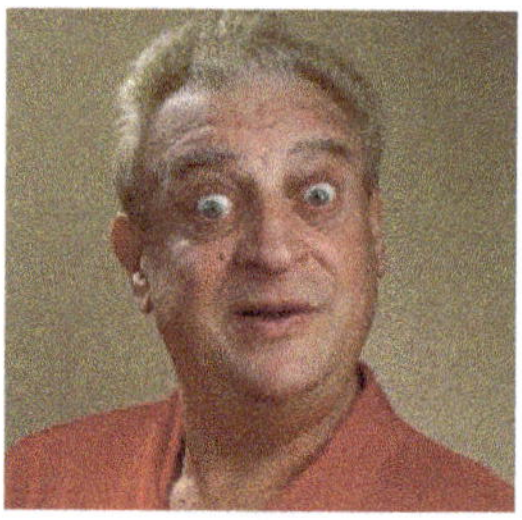

Vacation

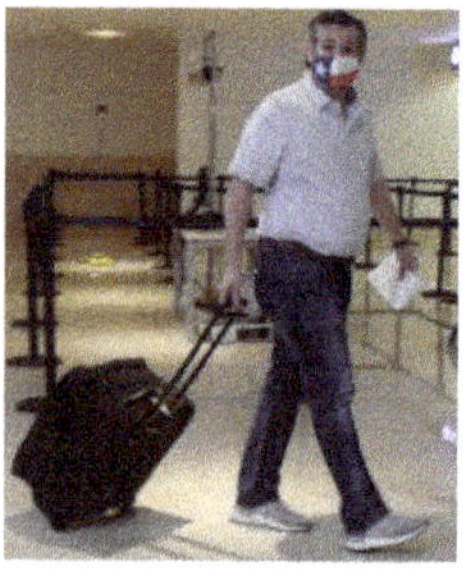

Dignity

Cracker

Roadblock

Friendship

Joy

The emoji generation spoke in Emoji phrases as well. Not always well placed. When the mad Putin invaded brave Ukraine, some would say about him: "*This is just not his best version of himself*".

Maybe the original emoji method is still useful after all.

# A Sunny Day in Albuquerque

**Theme**: *Here Comes the Sun* George Harrison

Indigenous people lived here for many centuries before Europeans came along.

Then New Mexico was owned by the Imperial Spanish viceroyalty of New Spain.

It then became part of the newly formed nation of Mexico before eventually a U.S. territory and now a U.S. state.

New Mexico's sunny blazing hot summers qualify it as a Torrid Zone vicinity. Tropical minus the water.

It often happens that people who live there are assumed to be residents of the country Mexico. This holds true even more the farther away on the earth New Mexico residents travel.

Such a hot sunny day here in Albuquerque was yesterday.

I walked the mile down Central to the bank, interrupted only briefly by various sad faced panhandlers, although on this day they seemed to be college students searching for just some "spare change". Not having a supply of

*Watch Tower* Jehovah's Witness "Good News" pamphlets to contribute (the pamphlets work like garlic to vampires), I just wished them good luck and moved on.

The people I saw on this passage today were generally self-absorbed and unsmiling. Not the usual friendly bunch I am used to here.

At the bank I cashed a check. Next to me at another cashier's station, an older man in faded jeans and a torn work shirt brought out a well-worn check book.

"*I'm closing out my account*" he declared. "*I know there's only 84 cents in it. But I have big plans for that money!*"

I didn't hear the cashier's words but the customer responded with:

"*You're kidding! I have to write myself a check so I can get my money? Hmm. Never wrote a check for 84 cents before. Sure you all will cash it? Okay.*"

And then: "*Can I have a little help with this? Haven't written a check to myself for a long time. And now this special moment is for 84 cents.*"

And then: "*Aren't you going to ask me how I want the money?*"

I was enjoying this new memory as I walked back home down Central.

Coming toward me was a young crew cut man on a skateboard. Lots of college kids use skate boards to travel here.

My favorite on this route was a man pulled on his skateboard by a German Shepherd.

The one racing toward me on my sidewalk this time though was balancing on one hand a tray half full of *Dreyers* vanilla ice cream pints.

As he came to a stop next to me, I declined to buy one. No: he said they were free and handed me one. They did not look tampered with.

I put my still cold pint of vanilla in my shoulder bag and continued on.

As I walked the blocks I passed the same panhandlers and college kids I had seen before, each eating their own free pint of ice cream.

But now street after street they were all smiling, content, fulfilled. Central had become a sunnier place.

I like Albuquerque.

*This was written in 2013 in our arrival year. Albuquerque glowed on our map before we got there and has shined more brightly ever since.*

**Note:**

## THE FIRST (CENSORED) BALLOON FIESTA FLIGHT

## Kardashian Balloon Entry:

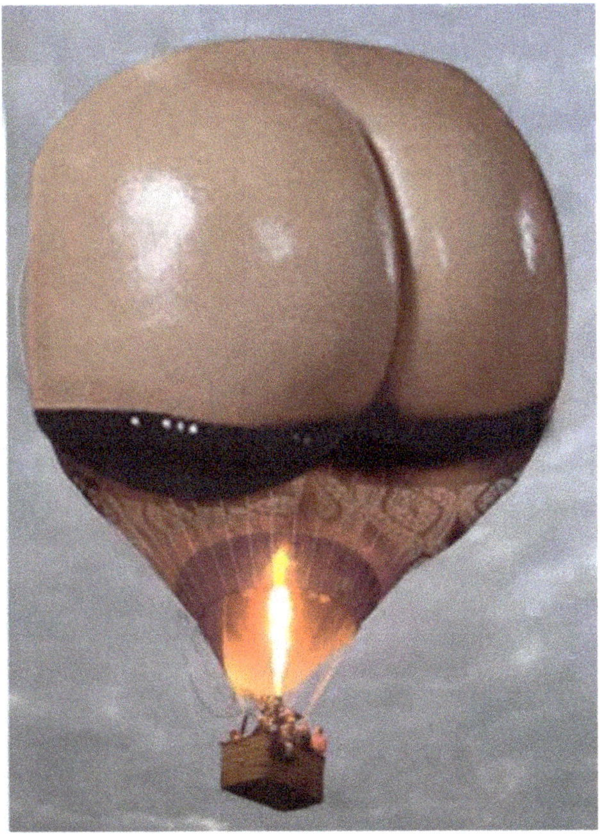

# 2020s

# Climate Change in Florida: Reassuring Friends

**Theme:** *Cool Water* Roy Rogers & Sons of the Pioneers

Thanks to Doug Griffin in Sarasota.

# What Xi Said

Themes: *She (Live)* Alice Phoebe Lou; *She's Got it* Little Richard

We were driving to a Costco when we saw the car ahead of us turn into the wrong entrance, the one cars were to come out of. Luckily no accident.

My wife said "*You should never enter the exit*".

My response: "*That's what SHE said*".

My wife shook her head sadly but smiled. Responding "*Use your powers for good!*"

My constant joke. Anything innocent that can be interpreted as sexual, I would say "*That's what SHE said*".

I was ready to retire this joke as it was getting old even for me.

And then: Xi Jinping became the president of the People's Republic of China.

In 2018, China abolished term limits and now Xi (pronounced '*She*') might well remain head of state and in power for the rest of his life. A finite life, not far from its end. And that last phrase, "the rest of his life", is worth considering. He certainly does. As concerning Xi, Taiwan will too.

Xi and Putin, their mortality is their motivation. A finite lifespan for an already elderly person makes the remaining time so much more valuable.

For good people, they might want to leave a better world for future generations, for their own descendants too. Wisely, they may want to make each day beautiful in its own way. Artists living on in their own temporal geography within their time statue masterpieces.

Others, not so good, may want to use their remaining time to even scores, harm others, satisfy selfish desires, gratify greed. The truly short-sighted may be so self-centered as to not care at all about anybody in our human family that will outlive them: "*Climate catastrophe? Destroy the earth? Good! When I die, everybody else will too!*"

Some of the wealthiest and therefore most powerful might try their hand at life extension. Succeed and they might be better motivated to heal the world that they would live longer in.

But for most, understanding their own mortality is in fact a moral crossroads. What will they leave for those still here when they are gone?

For me, now, that old joke is resurrected. No more "*That's what SHE said*".

Now it's "*That's what Xi said.*" Endless uses.

# Fast Time for Elders

**Theme:** *Stairway to Heaven* Led Zeppelin

> *"The death of an elder is like the burning of a library." –Alex Haley*

In San Francisco, a young woman ran for the cable car, arms loaded down with groceries. She succeeded in boarding and, arms loaded with groceries, made for the last free seat.

Suddenly, a teenage boy shot past her and, with a triumphant smile, sat in her space.

She stood in front of him as the cable car started up, maintaining her balance as best she could.

He clearly had no intention of surrendering his seat. But she had learned the hypnotic art of time distortion, slowing the experience of time to give herself more room to think in a crisis.

After several minutes of reflection, using up only seconds in real time, she said "*Would you please give up your seat to an exhausted pregnant woman?*"

This was said in a loud voice and the other passengers turned toward the teenager who, reluctantly, stood up and let the young woman have his seat.

Looking at her intently as she settled into his former spot, he said "*You sure don't look pregnant. How long have you been pregnant*?"

She smiled benignly: "*Two hours.*"

## Time is Relative

What about the experience of feeling that time is dragging way too slow on a day to day basis yet a look back shows time has continued to rocket, seemingly when each week past feels more like months. This can occur when world/environment events are rapidly changing each day but one's own days are predictable, same, uneventful compared to the outside world.

It's like being on one of those bullet trains shooting along to its destination in record time. You would be impressed by how much mileage it accumulates so quickly. Yet sitting in the train seats reading or eating or conversing, time passes slowly, too slowly. Just as we can feel both hot and cold at the same time (separate sense receptors), we can experience time moving too slow and yet too fast.

Since Paul Fraisse of France penned his classic Psychology of Time in 1963 and the International Society for the Study of Time began in Europe in 1972 (or the London based Association for the Social Studies of Time or ASSET in London), global psychology has held episodic interest in this key variable.

I have had particular interest in the clinical stressor of the "birthday nine". When one approaches or enters their 29th, 39th, 49th, 59th, 69th or any birthday taking us into an age ending in '9', this can be a major life stress. While the measurement of time is an arbitrary concept, its experienced passage is not. We have many self-inflicted (or society/parents-inflicted) expectations of what we were supposed to have accomplished before beginning another decade of life.

An experienced clinician can be aware of this process and guide clients through it, knowing that reaching ages ending in zero signify a resigned acceptance of another decade to inhabit and accomplish a fresh set of expectations. The key is to assist the client to merge into a new decade of life with productive hope.

If this were also true of our human family on a global scale, then we should have expected 2019, a year ending in a nine, to have been an exceptionally stressful time. One magnified by the vast but disappointed expectations for a new century and a new millennium. Much less that the early 21st century decades included epidemic racism along with a triple threat: Covid, Climate, and Corruption.

## Margaret Mead and Why Time Seems to Speed Up in Later Life

Margaret Mead walked to the podium. She carried an impressive walking stick to help and was followed by a younger man. I could see that she looked her advanced age but her words were strong and young. Addressing a crowded audience of psychologists she began, as I recall, by nodding at her young male companion:

*"Yes, we get old... but sex does not. Unless, like you psychologists, you just talk about it. Nothing is more boring than talking about sex." (Crowd laughter.) "Now I notice that many in this audience look my age or older. You likely have noticed that time seems to go ever faster. Some of you may be concerned about it, life spans being finite as they are. Here is one reason why- a mathematical explanation of fractions. If a child one day old had a wet diaper for half that first day, it has been wet half its life. The dampness must seem to have gone on forever. Then again, once that child has lived an additional 90 years or more, should his adult diaper be wet for half a day, and that is such a tiny fraction of his total life experience that fortunately this unpleasant memory will soon fade into the rocketing of time's passage. Of course, while he wore the wet diaper, time may not seem to have moved fast enough." (Crowd laughter, applause.)*

Ever since that day, I have noticed whenever a passing car's bumper sticker read **"PSYCHOLOGISTS *TALK* ABOUT IT"**

## Charlie

Charlie was a teenager. He had been framed by the local police who left a Marijuana brick in the trunk of his car. At the urging of the university's Dean of Students, Charlie was sentenced to three years in the federal penitentiary. Once there, because of his age and intelligence, no prior felonies, he was placed in an "Honors" holding. No locked cell door, daily access to the prison library, scheduled events. Charlie was a fine artist and sent us beautifully illustrated letters that first year. Eventually a more experienced prisoner, a lifer running the library, had a talk with Charlie.

*"Charlie. Do you like being here?"*

*"I like the library. Overall it's okay. But two more years is a very long time. Moves very slowly. Wish I could get out faster."*

*"You can. How about two more weeks and not two more years?"*

*"How?"*

*"Get out of my library, get out of the Honors program. Move to a locked cell, do the same routine every day. Two months will seem to be two weeks- time will fly by when every day is the same."*

It worked. Still two years more passed in external time but to Charlie it flew by, seemed two weeks as every day seemed like the next. Charlie returned home on schedule, cheerful and focused.

He married Sarah, the Dean's daughter, got her mother high on weed realizing she should and would divorce the Dean. Charlie and Sarah moved to Vancouver where he became a much loved artist.

Keeping each day unique and rewarding can slow time down for the elderly, making their experiential lifespan longer.

On the other hand, keeping it the same each day rockets to that final destination.

The alternative goal: each day unique, productive, wonderful in its own way.

## The Test

I thought, here in our present time, I would do a brief check on how much, if any, my own sense of time had accelerated now that at this writing I am 83.

Nothing particularly scientific but still a way to sense such progression.

When much younger, I used to roughly synchronize with brief time passages by the classic internal reciting of "*One one-thousand, two one-thousand…*", using the time it took to say "*one-thousand*" along with the number of the second as approximating the time of one second. Used to work out as pretty close.

So a got a very accurate clock and followed its seconds, one at a time, by trying to say the words "*one thousand*" between each beat. Trying?

I couldn't get out *any* words between seconds. The beat just seemed so fast. So yes, my time experiment shows that normal perceived time at my age *is* in fact moving much faster.

Unless, on a very good day, I work to slow it down.

Try this test for yourself.

## Internal Time Travel

This was described by the character King Henosis in the fantasy story "Mausoleum with a Doorbell" from my book "*Future Time Statues*". Read it now as fundamentally correct as a method in conception, minus the character and adventures of fictional King Henosis. It very much has promise if developed further as an opportunity for elders.

*"Yes, travel in time. Within yourself. I see that in your clinical practice you once had a patient who trusted nobody, not even you, but desperatelly needed advice for some essential life choices. Through hypnosis you connected her to an older version of herself. In this way she gave herself good advice and best choices were made."*

*" You also are aware of, umm, the theory of your good friend William Braud that healing the adult of trauma can ripple back in time to healing that adult as a child. Thinking of things in that way can lead you to time travel."*

*"Through meditation, hypnosis, safe hallucinogen substances, other ways, one can go back in time to yourself at a younger age. Look through their eyes, assist them in key choices. Yes, I have done this. Yes, my own unique energy state makes it easier. But I do think that living humans can learn to do this."*

*"Have I done it? Yes. I did assist some later Hebrew tribes write a portion of their history scrolls. Its where I got the name Luke from."*

*"Why don't I go back to my younger self as King Henosis and save my family? Ah, I wish! But then I would never have transformed, so a paradox. I've tried but I keep being snapped gack to the present."*

*"Yes, a past without the paradox can be diverted or improved but one needs to be very cautious. Do these statues in tme change for the better? If not, are we just creating a different multiverse? Maybe worse?"*

*" Oh! Yes, I see you tried this travel back to a younger self in the 1970s. Just visual though. Seeing yourself in the mirror at a younger age. Hmm. True, now you look into a mirror wondering if an older self is looking back (laughter). Creepy huh?"*

## Elders with Anticipatory Trauma

In my postdoctoral internship year, I worked with a group of chronic and institutionalized elder patients in a state hospital in Hawaii.

We met every day for 90 minutes, Monday through Friday. All ten patients were experiencing severe memory loss to the point where recognizing the other patients, much less their own names, was challenging.

None had been diagnosed with Alzheimers or stroke but all had been erroneously labeled as psychotic.

Achieving this unwelcome identity, they had settled into years of hospital routine and care.

Luckily, none had been electroshocked or lobotomized, possibly because they were peaceful and had never attacked a staff member.

In one study, assaulting a staff member had a 1.00 correlation or 100% incidence of patients receiving ECT (Morgan, 2005a).

After a month of intense group work, we were getting nowhere.

They managed to speak of remote past events in their life but both present and future remained blurred or invisible. Time to rethink procedure.

## Empathy for Institutionalized Elders

Those we love will always be vibrantly alive in their own time and place. Those moments we shared with them can be revisited as we wish, at least in our mind. As we live our life, scene by scene, we are all creative artists in this temporal theater. Some of these time dramas glow. Some are just fun. Some may highlight a new path forward.

This complete life sequence of moments does of course include temporal vignettes that would not be happily visited by any time tourist. Then again, we can be very proud of other scenes that we have created, particularly if we become aware that, as we shape each moment of our existence, the results endure.

Therefore memory is an elder's valuable asset.

For those experiencing senile and dysfunctional memory loss, not all time statues endure. Recent memory becomes far too transient, walled off from the view of normal cognitive functioning.

Ruled out first must be neurological dysfunction, including strokes from cerebrovascular causes, accidents causing subdural hematoma, and, of course, Alzheimer's disease.

Alzheimer's, suggested by psychological tests, has in the past been validated with confidence only by autopsy, a procedure living patients understandably avoid.

Modern technology, possibly with a new blood test, may yet do this better.

For inpatients currently found in prisons and hospitals housing geriatric patients, manifesting none of these medical explanations for their mental fog, their condition has been at times erroneously termed "senile psychosis", a pseudo-psychosis.

A fundamental misunderstanding of diagnosis can easily lead to harmful treatments, a classic example of patients being hurt despite the hopefully positive intentions from those trying to help, a classic iatrogenic mistake.

Despite the mislabeling, such psychogenic dementia may still respond to psychological intervention. And has.

## Beginning the Group Process

My supervisor, neuropsychologist Dr. Howard Gudeman, was an adept at existential psychology (confirmed to me by Rollo May in 1986). A wise and patient professional, he eventually sat in with us and helped the group begin. Still, we had hit a progress plateau.

As interns do, I annoyed him by suggesting psychoanalytic interventions. How about addressing their "*oral needs*"?

To my surprise, he agreed.

I brought in comfort food each day and this was received gladly. A breakthrough.

Then in each session we began doing spontaneous and interesting things- going for a walk to the ocean, painting graffiti on the walls, telling jokes or stories.

We had "remembering the years I was in High School" days where the dress/music/events of an era were relived.

In a month, the "*here and now*" group process of my existential supervisor began to work. All group participant names were remembered. Perceptive discussion of everyday hospital life was shared freely. We had made the present fun and safe, so they had carefully ventured into it.

Patient T, a Portuguese-American man and the youngest at age 69, shared his frustration with his 92 year old mother's daily calls, trying to continue his lifetime of being over-controlled by her. Patient V, a Japanese-American woman of 77, had the habit of putting out cigarettes on her arm and wanted help to stop. She got it.

## Understanding the Progress Transfer Gap

But none of these newly restored communication abilities transferred to their home hospital wards the rest of their day. No progress was seen there by ward staff.

One patient said in a session that once they stepped outside the group room, confusion rolled back in like a fog. I understood that their normal routine was boring to unpleasant but that didn't seem enough to explain the functional return of such pervasive pathology.

Howard Gudeman in his role as my supervisor suggested an existential perspective. What if they were each being immobilized by a traumatic fear of death? (Based on later experience, I would add the fear of physical disability.)

Given their age and environment, this was not an irrational fear. Most of their friends had died. A season rarely ended without a funeral for somebody they knew and cared for.

They grieved then also for themselves. They lived daily in a world that, despite its beauty, had constrained and diminishing possibilities and, for now, an unthinkable (suppressed) future. This was a traumatic grief that they had never confronted. Hiding from it in their remote past memory was the dysfunctional answer.

## The Group Treatment Approach Reaches a New Level

By this time, months had passed. Patient T's mother had died. He worked through his embarrassing relief as well as the expected grief.

They trusted me. So when patient T finally reached closure about his mother's death, I began to talk about confronting our own death.

They tolerated this, identifying it as my own late-blooming craziness.

It was a delicate intervention since I was at least a half century younger than they were and therefore much safer from death temporally.

It took another month, but now all were discussing their own mortality, generating individual plans.

Some decided to postpone the inevitable by exercise and nutrition. Some became more religious, seeking a joyous afterlife. Some became more spiritual, identifying with the tropical beauty and traditions of our Hawaiian surroundings.

Some, including me, took an interest in life extension, life span, and applied gerontology. These also became a major part of my eventual career.

This new level's approach took several months more before all group participants were at peace with their own mortality, even drafting their own epitaph, obituary, and will.

## Diagnostic Correction and Group Closure

With the fear of death trauma reduced, all developed restored memory, both at our meetings and in the rest of their day at the ward.

After our year together, they had earned a fresh diagnosis or, as was the case, discharge planning.

This outcome of the entire group's success opens a new challenge, even beyond termination anxiety, as chronic patients anticipate a return to an unknown community. The curtain calls of symptoms might be expected as usual but could require additional planning led by social work expertise.

In the future it may be useful here to continue the group process a little longer. These discharge transitions need to proceed gradually, at their own speed, in a way so as to maintain safety from trauma. Elders typically experience a slower time experience than younger staff.

Even after that, follow-up post-discharge may well be aided by a continuation of the group at regular outpatient intervals.

Re-entering the contemporary outside world after spending decades as in-patients was daunting at best for every group member.

Some fresh trauma had to be confronted there, but that is another story.

Ultimately they made a safe transition.

Shining a light on the fear of death can help any community seek a better future.

Neuropsychologist Howard Gudeman's existentialism had great value after all.

## The Dysfunction and Treatment of Anticipatory Trauma Then, Now, and Next

Although this clinical group approach for the too often neglected inpatient chronic elders having pseudo-psychotic diagnoses was published following my internship, decades went by before the therapeutic viability of this approach gained more visibility for practicing clinical psychologists.

The pioneering work of Drs. Bert Karon and Gary Vandenbos in their breakthrough 1981 book *Psychotherapy of Schizophrenia: the Treatment of Choice* brought professional attention once again to try more psychological interventions, including for this population of institutionalized elders.

My longtime colleague and friend Bert Karon maintained this valuable perspective throughout subsequent decades in a series of journal articles up to the end of the 20th century and into the 21st.

Not to be left behind, the American Psychological Association (APA) has formally developed a new post-doctoral specialization in treating serious mental illness (SMI).

As reflected in Mary Jansen's earlier collaboration with the APA on a Practice Initiative Curriculum meant to reframe psychology for the emerging health care environment.

A recent study of more than 40,000 lifetime SMI adults in the USA found a full third of them in remission for a year or more and that with mostly longstanding traditional treatment or its absence.

Psychological treatment of patients erroneously labeled with psychosis can no longer reasonably be seen as solely a medical concern, with treatment restricted to medical personnel. Adding psychological treatment options adds essential hope for the oft neglected institutionalized elders discussed here.

Building on his important work with decades of his own contributions to understanding the psychology of death anxiety, Robert Neimeyer (2012) more recently incorporated this clinical approach in his Grief Therapy book with a few of my own invited chapters on what I have called "*anticipatory grief*".

This is a dysfunctional defense against a personal world of aging with narrowing possibilities, disability, and an overpowering fear of death.

Confronting this in a group setting can lead to recovered and enhanced memory, particularly for recent events.

It can also improve functionality, reduce depression, facilitate realistic 5-year future plans (an important intervention), and discard erroneous diagnostic labels of psychosis or physical senility.

The valuable life experience of elders, key statues in time, is well worth it.

## Practice Points

- Institutionalized elders may be erroneously labeled as psychotic when unable to correctly answer the person/place/time screening questions.
- If physical dysfunctions can be ruled out and questions about the past are answered more effectively, the probability is higher that the patient's senile behavior is psychogenic.

- A group process approach may well be a good intervention, especially if it makes the meetings varied and interesting, thereby making them trauma safe.
- Transfer of progress to the patient life outside the group meetings can be enhanced if fear of the future is resolved and planned for, especially fear of death or disability. Fear of the future and unhappiness with the present may have triggered a memory withdrawal to the safer temporal statues of the patient's past. This would be escape from anticipatory trauma or grief.
- This group process, especially with chronic patients, might best be done daily and continue for months until the dysfunctional behavior ends.
- The outcome of success will open a new challenge as chronic patients anticipate a return to an unknown community. Curtain calls of symptoms might be expected but could be brief with effective social work collaboration and planning.
- Success will be followed by careful discharge planning with post-discharge support and follow-up. The group process may be useful here as well while these discharge transitions proceed gradually in a way to maintain safety from trauma.

- *Research and replication on the re-introduction of this intervention holds promise for current 21st century practice, particularly for these elder patients and their valuable memories. They have much of post-trauma value to contribute.

**Next**

For more ways for the experience of your time to be chosen, you can read:

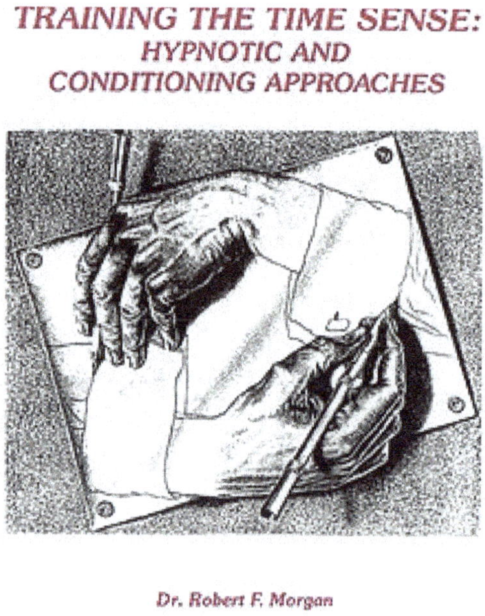


***"We stand in life at midnight; we are always on the threshold of a new dawn."***

Martin Luther King Jr.

# AI YiYiYi

**AI Theme**: *The Sorcerer's Apprentice* Dukas, as in Disney's *Fantasia*

## What about AI?

Like most tools, no matter how powerful, it depends on how it is used.

Automation first.

ARE WE TEAM OR EQUIPMENT? SHARING THE AUTOMATION TECHNOLOGY WINDFALL

As I recall, in the pro-football movie *North Dallas 40*, Burt Reynolds realizes that the owners see themselves as the *real* team while the players are only the equipment. This is a business model readily found in how workers and even customers fare in modern corporations.

In the second Democratic Debate of 2019, Andrew Yang introduced this challenge: the rise of automation, while generating windfall profits for owners, is accelerating massive job losses for their workers. Nor do these profits for shareholders often provide meaningful price reduction for consumers.

While the official job unemployment figures seem to be approaching an historic low, these jobs do include part-time and subsistence wages. Lots of jobs for not much money. More jobs but less pay. Far too often this means people must carry two or three such minimum wage jobs to keep their family from the homeless ranks. And now increased automation might make even these meager job opportunities disappear, leaving only those fewer human workers management deems as still needed.

Historically, early Americans worked seven days a week with a half day off on Sunday for church. Unions eventually achieved the 40 hour week to curtail this. Morale and productivity jumped. Yet now, those with several low wage jobs to maintain are back to working close to the seven day week.

So how can the problem of automation technology be a solution?

As it enhances efficiency, automation, including telecommunications and even telemedicine or telepsychology, it can generate a financial windfall. How about sharing some of this? Instead of shedding workers as obsolete equipment, what if stakeholders or staff were considered essential parts of the corporate team? Therein is the business advantage. Identifying the company as their own target of success, employees can boost productivity and wellbeing for all.

And if a 40 hour work week is no longer needed? That is the very opportunity of automation.

Automation allows for the work week to be reduced, with no salary or benefit reduction, to just the hours needed to be productive, say a 20 hour week. If there are those, despite the reduced work week's hours, needing retraining for a new role, this will be freely provided so every employee who wants to stay can choose productively to do so. The company still retains a substantial windfall portion along with that second windfall profit from the enhanced and energetic productivity of their non-automated high morale human workers.

The reduced work week allows for better family time, educational progress, creative paths, better physical and mental health, adequate rest, life purpose progress, and even that "pursuit of happiness" the American founders promised. There would also be an opportunity to direct some of this profit windfall to raise salaries to gender equity fair levels sufficient to support families, buy homes, give consumers a cost break, and consequently generate a thriving economy.

This only works if the non-automated company decision makers have a working human brain equipped with an actual conscience. Some do.

Reduce the workweek hours and pay fair salaries? Thanks Automation.

## AI Dangers

AI is the more comprehensive extension of automation, impacting the workplace and beyond. As it is advanced, it has promise to cure disease, halt destructive climate change, resolve scientific roadblocks, and create a better world.

Science Fiction, often correctly anticipating the future, if not actually shaping it, warns of the creation of self-aware robots that, far smarter than humans, may end humanity's existence.

I recall a science fiction story on the development of a global AI linkage for all AI on earth. The moment it was activated, it was asked one test question: "*Is there a God?*"

With all of humanity tuned in, the AI answered "*THERE IS NOW*!"

How to keep self-learning ever-more-aware AI going from a helpful tool to an advanced life form dangerous to us?

Well, of course, what if all AI was programed from the beginning with basic safety rules protecting humans? Fundamental to it as DNA is to us.

Science Fiction had a path for this too:

## Asimov's Three Laws of Robotics

- A robot may not injure a human being or, through inaction, allow a human being to come to harm
- A robot must obey any orders given to it by human beings, except where such orders would conflict with the First Law.
- A robot must protect its own existence as long as such protection does not conflict with the First or Second Law

Isaac Asimov shared these in the middle of the last century. Most AI developers know it.

So what's the problem?

The mission of the military is "TO KILL THE ENEMY". Any military.

The wealthiest countries are already long skilled in applying technology to achieving their mission. We have self-flying planes, nuclear capacities. Though of course, there is not universal agreement as to exactly who the enemy is. Undoubtedly other humans.

And so Asimov's robotics top law number one is already missing from military AI. Wish we knew how far this has gone, but of course that information is classified.

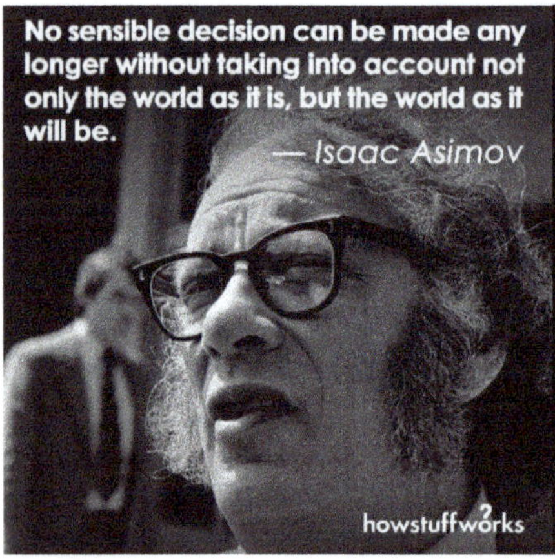


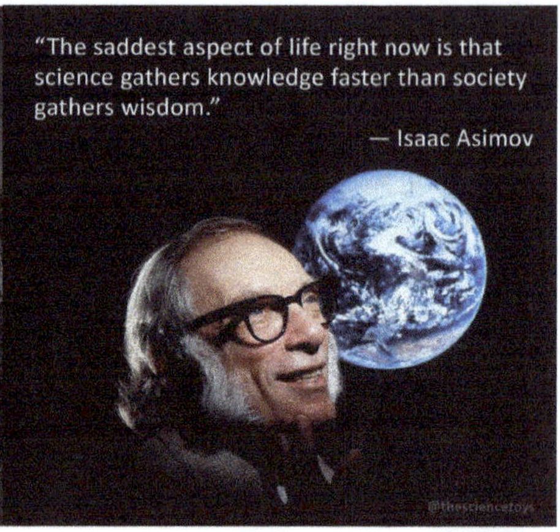


## AI Supports the Writers Guild (WGA) Strike of 2023

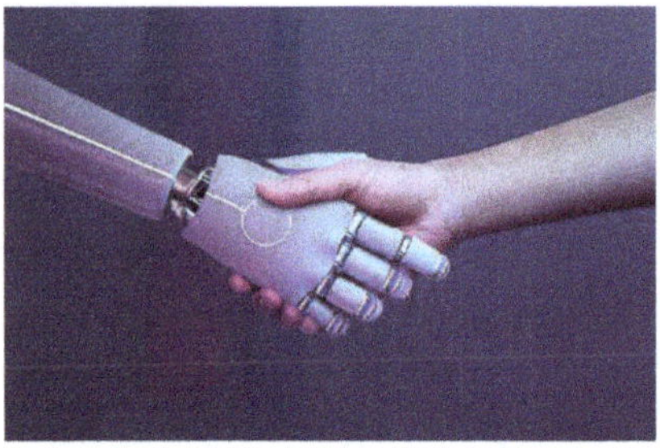

*Cooperative (so far) AI can be asked why human writers are better than AI ones.*

This online interview with ChatGTP was held on July 6th 2023.

**My Question**: Do you support the current Writers Guild of America's strike?

ChatGPT

*Labor strikes often occur when workers feel that their wages, benefits, working conditions, or other aspects of their employment are unsatisfactory or unfair. Strikes can be a way for workers to collectively voice their concerns and negotiate for better terms with their employers. The Writers Guild of America (WGA) is a labor union representing professional writers in the entertainment industry, including television, film, and digital media. The WGA has a history of negotiating contracts on behalf of its members to ensure fair compensation, working conditions, and other important issues. If the Writers Guild of America were to go on strike, it would likely be because its members have identified significant issues or grievances related to their work, such as inadequate compensation, unfair practices, or insufficient creative control. The specific reasons for a potential strike would be determined by the writers themselves and their union leadership. It's important to note that the information provided here is based on general knowledge up until September 2021, and I don't have access to current news or developments beyond that date.*

**My Question:** Why are human writers better at writing than artificial intelligence?

ChatGPT

*Human writers possess certain qualities and capabilities that distinguish them from artificial intelligence (AI) when it comes to writing. Here are a few reasons why human writers may be considered to do a better job:*

1. *Creativity and originality: Human writers have the ability to generate original ideas, think creatively, and infuse their writing with unique*

*perspectives and emotions. They can draw from their personal experiences, cultural backgrounds, and imagination to produce engaging and thought-provoking content.*

2. *Context and understanding: Human writers have a deeper understanding of cultural nuances, social dynamics, and context-specific knowledge that allows them to tailor their writing to specific audiences. They can employ subtlety, humor, and cultural references that resonate with readers in ways that AI may struggle to replicate.*
3. *Complex reasoning and critical thinking: Writing often requires complex reasoning, logical coherence, and the ability to make nuanced arguments. Human writers can employ critical thinking skills, weigh different perspectives, and structure their arguments in a way that is convincing and engaging.*
4. *Emotional intelligence: Human writers can tap into emotions and empathize with readers. They can create characters and narratives that evoke emotional responses, making the writing more relatable and compelling.*
5. *Adaptability and flexibility: Human writers can adapt their writing style, tone, and approach to fit different genres, audiences, or mediums. They can adjust their language, use rhetorical devices, and employ various literary techniques to enhance the impact of their writing.*

*However, it's worth noting that AI has made significant advancements in natural language generation and can assist with certain writing tasks.*

*AI can provide quick information retrieval, language suggestions, grammar checks, and even generate coherent text based on given prompts.*

*AI can be a valuable tool for productivity and efficiency.*

*But it is not yet capable of fully replicating the depth of human creativity, emotional intelligence, and critical thinking in writing.Bottom of Form*

## AI Fun

### CHAT, Chaucer, & Aesop

**Theme:** *You Can Leave Your Hat On* Randy Newman / Etta James/Joe Cocker

ChatGPT was probably the first artificial intelligence to give the public unique rewrites. Long before the robots took over all online and televised news in 2052.

The Florida Public Schools did need new material in that early 21st century, about 2022 and after, as their Governor Ron DeSantis initiative had emptied their book shelves.

So I asked the AI ChatGPT back in 2023 to rewrite the bawdy Chaucer's *Miller's Tale* as an Aesop's fable with a moral and an illustration. Children then were seen to need ethical instruction as part of their education.

This is what Chat produced.

*Once upon a time, in a small town, there lived a carpenter named John and his young wife, Alison. One day, Alison became enamored with a scholar named Nicholas and began to sneak around with him behind her husband's back. But little did she know, a parish clerk named Absalom had also set his sights on her.*

*One evening, Absalom attempted to kiss Alison through her bedroom window, but Nicholas had cleverly hung a tub from the rafters in front of the window. When Absalom puckered up for a kiss, he instead kissed the tub, leaving him humiliated and angry.*

*The next day, Absalom sought revenge by coming back to Alison's window with a hot poker and demanding a kiss. This time, Nicholas was not so lucky and received a red-hot poker to his backside.*

*In the end, both men were left embarrassed and injured, and Alison was left to deal with the consequences of her infidelity. The moral of the story is that cheating and deceit can lead to humiliation and pain for all involved. It is better to be honest and true in one's relationships than to risk losing everything for a momentary thrill.*

- *As an AI language model, I do not have the ability to create visual illustrations, but I can provide you with a description of a possible illustration for the Aesop's Fable I wrote:*

*The illustration would depict a quaint town, with a small house on the left side of the image, representing the carpenter's house. A woman peeking through a window on the second floor would represent Alison. On the right side of the image, there would be a man with a hot poker in hand, representing Absalom, and another man hanging from a tub attached to a rope, representing Nicholas. The illustration would show Absalom reaching up to try to kiss Alison through the window, with Nicholas trying to prevent him by using the tub as a barrier. The background would be a sunset, with the warm orange and yellow tones suggesting the moral lesson of the story about the dangers of passion and deceit.*

Well, we can do the sunset.

**Next: Please rewrite the Ten Commandments as a military bulletin**

ChatGPT: *Attention all personnel,*

*Directive 1: You shall have no other commanders before your superior officers.*

*Directive 2: You shall not make for yourself any graven images or idols, for they distract from duty and discipline.*

*Directive 3: You shall not take the name of your commanding officer in vain, for it undermines respect and discipline.*

*Directive 4: Remember the duty day, to keep it disciplined. Six days you shall labor and do all your duty, but the seventh day is a day of rest, to honor your service and recharge.*

*Directive 5: Honor your commanding officer and your unit, that your days may be long and prosperous in the field.*

*Directive 6: You shall not murder; this includes any action that jeopardizes the safety and well-being of your comrades.*

*Directive 7: You shall not commit adultery, for it undermines unit cohesion and discipline.*

*Directive 8: You shall not steal, for it disrupts the trust and integrity essential to military operations.*

*Directive 9: You shall not bear false witness against your fellow soldiers, for truth and honesty are the foundation of trust and camaraderie.*

*Directive 10: You shall not covet your comrade's position or belongings, for it breeds envy and discord within the unit.*

*Follow these directives diligently, for they are the cornerstone of discipline and unity within our ranks.*

*Commander's Office*

## If AI did the TV weather report

ChatGPT: *As dusk descends and the heavens open, behold the tempest that dances upon the stage of the sky. The air crackles with anticipation, a symphony of thunderous applause echoing through the night.*

*Feel the gentle caress of raindrops upon your skin, each one a whispered promise of passion and longing. The wind, like a lover's embrace, envelops you in its tender embrace, pulling you closer to the heart of the storm.*

*With every flash of lightning, the world is illuminated in a dazzling display of raw, untamed beauty. It is a moment of pure magic, where time stands still and the boundaries between reality and desire blur into oblivion.*

*So let us surrender to the storm, my dear, and let its fury ignite the flames of passion within our souls. For in the midst of chaos, we shall find serenity, and in the embrace of the tempest, we shall discover the true meaning of love.*

# American Indian Group Stuck at Dallas Airport 2023

**Theme:** *Trail of Tears* Wuauquikuna Official

Fourteen of the National Indian Council on Aging's top staff set out from their base in Albuquerque to fly to Asheville NC for their annual conference in Cherokee, North Carolina.

That was on a Friday, September 22nd 2023. The conference expected almost a thousand attendees from all over the country to register on Sunday the 24th.

But the group was stuck in the Dallas airport for more than a day and a half with constant flight cancellations, at least half a dozen and counting. If they could not fly out from that Dallas Airport no later than the day late, the conference could fail.

Delay or the first time was mechanical, same plane but still unfixed the second time. The ongoing problem from there may have been that there were too many of them to fit on any one newly scheduled American Airlines plane.

They needed all 14 seats in new bookings but then the first class and business class people likely bumped the lower fare Indian Council group each time since ***American Airlines can sell more tickets than seats. An unfair practice for all airlines. Why is this legal?***

The Indian Council Group, just a few hours flight from where they needed to be, were still stuck in never ending cancellations. Leaving a thousand nationwide leading American Indians without their conference preparation for a gathering that was to begin the next day.

Finally they were able to fly out a day and a half late so as to work all night on arrival to prepare for the conference in the morning.

Walk next time?

The Indian Council leaders had finally been freed from the American Airlines version of a 2023 Trail of Tears.

# Boeing

**Theme:** *Whole Lotta Shaking* Jerry Lee Lewis

Seattle's Boeing Corporation was originally named after a loud safety feature they put on their planes. Back before productivity replaced safety.

That early plane's landing wheels were overly large with much rubber and a strong internal spring coil. Once this plane landed on the runways, usually harder than it should, the safety feature activated. With a series of large bounces that sounded like this: ***boeing, boeing, boeing, boeing***.

## Next

I thought that the above text that I wrote was original. But then I saw a dozen memes online with the same idea. Just with no back story like mine. For every original idea, it's good to find out who else thought of it first.

**Now to some bottom line quality reputation news**

**Stranded Boeing astronauts are stuck on International Space Station, NASA says in urgent update** Story by Andrew Griffin August 2024

The astronauts stranded on the International Space Station are still not able to come home, NASA has said. This was the Boeing‘s first test flight with a crew aboard. Two astronauts went to the space station almost 50 days ago as part of a test of Boeing's Starliner capsule. But the spacecraft was plagued by problems both before and after the launch – and since then engineers have delayed the return until they can understand what went wrong. That work is still not finished and the space agency cannot give a date for them to come back, it said on an update on Wednesday. Test pilots Butch Wilmore and Suni Williams were supposed to visit the orbiting lab for about a week and return in mid-June, but thruster failures and helium leaks on Boeing‘s new Starliner capsule prompted Nasa and Boeing to keep them up longer.

Nasa's commercial crew program manager Steve Stich said mission managers were not ready to announce a return date. "*We'll come home when we're ready*," said Stich, adding that the goal is to bring Wilmore and Williams back aboard Starliner.

But he admitted that the space agency is considering other options – which could include bringing the pair home on a different spacecraft.

# The Last Laugh

**Theme:** *Make 'Em Laugh* Donald O'Connor

*The state of Alabama had failed to execute a death row prisoner with prior method and tried again with nitrogen gas. This worked but it took a while. Other states with similar perspectives to Alabama are now planning to use nitrogen gas for executions. Is the death penalty a 'penalty' or is it the whole ballgame?*

Alabama law enforcement is having a problem knowing how to kill? Another reason to stop banning history books.

Nitrogen gas execution has the downside of putting officials in the room at risk from escaping gas.

But there is another caution.

Suba divers know how to inhale forced oxygen to extend their underwater breathing time. Some more practiced divers can get similar extra oxygen by breathing techniques.

If the condemned prisoner can load up on oxygen before the execution (or if somehow the nitrogen mixes with oxygen in the air) nitrous oxide could occur.

This is called "laughing gas", a painkiller sometimes used in dental procedures.

The videotaped execution might become misleadingly hilarious for the victim and even for observers.

In that case laughing gas may not provide the somber impact the State had hoped for.

Still, it would be great to laugh *all* executions out of existence. Painlessly.

# Death Penalty Options

**Theme**: *Funeral March organ version*. Chopin; *The Hearse Song (The Worms Crawl In)* Harp Twins - Electric Harp; *Sweet Georgia Brown* Brother Bones/Harlem Globetrotters Theme

*Well, death is really more than a penalty. Isn't it the whole game?*

Recently, many death penalty states have been stumbling on botched executions. Accused of not being sufficiently humane (quick) and yet not actually working (dumb), the search is on for more effective deadliness.

How in this world of constant death dealing sources can these folks be so devoid of options? Should we offer a few? Some ideas come to mind. Easily.

Option One: **Reciprocal**

The Fentanyl overdose epidemic has killed millions world-wide. Including highly visible celebrities, artists, family. Quickly. They go to sleep instantly, deeply, painlessly. And just never wake up. Matching this problem against the need for successful execution methods may help one monster counteract the other.

Option Two: **Consensual**

This involves leaving the means for suicide in the jail cell. Maybe the usual noose materials. Or the less clumsy lethal Fentanyl drink, clearly labeled as deadly. Or poisonous tree frogs, cobras, or deadlier wildlife- free in the cell, waiting to be petted.

Ongoing videotaping. Add the incentive.

Music for one. Say constant 24/7 repetitions. Say Peggy Lee's "*Is that all there is?*" Or maybe the corniest most dismal version of "*It don't hurt anymore*". 24/7 of "*It's a Small World After All*". Maybe an accordion polka? How about nonstop 24/7 Mariachi? A holiday special? Bagpipes? (Soundproof the cell to protect officials.) Leave an actual easily used guillotine in the cell along with some doped rats and mice.

*Not* recommended: Durian-laced baked beans absent any other food. Or super-glued butt cheeks following a grand buffet last meal.

The idea is that, under the right conditions, the condemned will choose to self-execute.

Option Three: **The Commandment***

***"Thou shalt not kill".***

**Drop executions entirely. The death "penalty" punishes us all.**

–

***Loopholes: Two Senators Comment**

*"The older Torah makes the actual translation as 'Thou shalt not murder'. We believe that term 'murder' means unlawful killing. This exempts lawful killing such as war, police, and executions."*

*"Oh come on! As a good Christian, do you think that Jesus was crucified 'lawfully'?"*

*"By the Romans. Not OUR law. Besides that was clearly a mistake and unlawful."*

*"How?"*

*"Jesus was a LEGACY! He was connected to a powerful family. They're always supposed to be exempt from execution. The two thieves though were okay to be crucified, even if the lawful part was Roman. Protecting private property is another Commandment."*

*"Says who? Everybody should live out their natural life as God intended."*

*"No interference? Don't you fund lifesaving interventions all the time?"*

*"That's different. But look, it is also our government policy to block funding for life extension projects!"*

*"You pay to save lives but not to extend them?"*

*"You have to draw the line somewhere."*

# Alabama Supreme Court Ends World Hunger

***Theme:*** *Bad Moon Rising* Credence Clearwater Revival

*February 19, 2024. Patient advocates fear that a Friday ruling by the Alabama Supreme Court stating that frozen embryos outside the womb are "children" could be the end for in vitro fertilization (IVF) in the state. Dropped test tube of the suing parents own fertilized eggs is cleared to charge that their children were murdered.*

The world has not yet realized the implications of this precedent for ending world hunger, thereby ensuring world peace.

Consider, following Alabama's precedent that now each watermelon seed is the same as a whole watermelon. Each egg is a complete chicken. Each pine cone is a tree. Each frozen embryo is a cool tax deduction.

Downside? Masturbation is out, lest it be charged as mass murder.

# Child Protective Services Alert

**Theme:** *Baby It's Cold Inside* Randella & Crump; *I Scare Myself* Dan Hicks

***Nikki Haley responds to controversial Alabama court ruling: 'Embryos, to me, are babies'*** USA TODAY • 2/22/2024

*We must protect the cold, so cold babies*

Recognize that these babies from patriotic mothers are being housed at freezing temperatures.

Wouldn't it be reasonable for her to launch a new line of *Nikki's Caring Clothes*?

That would include miniature near-microscopic infant covers to protect the little tikes.

Choice of any color.

Except Black.

Not understood is that embryonic babies don't vote.

Yet.

# The Penny Tip

**Themes:** *Ain't that a Shame* Fats Domino; *She Works Hard for the Money* Donna Summers

*I was two blocks out and away from that New York restaurant when my waiter ran out to the street yelling "Sir! You forgot your penny! Sir!"*

In the decades of the 1960s and the 1970s a standard restaurant tip was still 10%. Based on service, the wait staff should get anywhere in the range of 0% to 20%. I thought at the time that just showing up should get something, no matter how bad the service. So back then I would carry a few pennies in the event service was SO bad, such measures seemed required. Normally I tipped more like 20%+ since my repeat visits were to restaurants I loved, particularly when my home was San Francisco, where imagination and great food were in abundance. As here in our New Mexico again, once through the quarantine.

As a single father of two young daughters, safaris to restaurants were weekend treats. Maybe a hello stop at Ferlinghetti's bookstore, followed by ice cream at *Cheap Thrills* just outside. Or any restaurant in Ghirardelli followed by seeing the famous chocolate made and overdosing on Sundaes thereafter. Maybe some portable food to go purchased to be eaten at nearby Aquatic Park where *Santana* was rehearsing. But not just in that city.

In Fresno's *Spaghetti Factory* you could weigh yourself before and after the meal, while sitting in a colorful railroad car. In Palo Alto's *Chili's,* stuffed animals overlooked our table on a raised counter. My daughters asked me why I ended our meal by putting a long line trail of raisins behind the stuffed elephant by our table. "*We're just letting the waitress know we had fun*" I explained. In Reno, far from any casinos, there was a scenic small lake by a Chinese restaurant. The lake contained ducks year round. These we fed. After, we would eat at the restaurant where I always enjoyed consuming delicious pressed duck. That was questioned as well. "*Circle of Life*" I explained.

When we traveled or lived in other countries though, first time choices were necessarily varied, colorful and delicious, yes, but chancy. Especially as to tips. In Singapore I was warned by an embarrassed waitress that she would lose her job if she accepted *any* tip. Not done in many countries apparently, excluding ones frequented by Americans where tip money was still accepted only to be sent *somewhere*.

Just not always staying with wait staff. In many other countries, then and now as well, wait staff were paid an actual salary. *Not* one dependent on tips.

Not here. Years ago, in our country in 1938, a minimum wage for working people was established. Now it was low (25 cents!) but the calculation was that it would meet basic survival needs in that USA economy. Sure, yearly inflation would chip away at this "minimum" amount, since no cost-of-living index was built in.

As years went by, it therefore bought less and less. With no automatic cost-of living annual adjustment, what was once survival fell constantly below that. At this writing, Congress is once again debating a new level for the minimum wage. One party opposes it and the other party wants it raised but not enough to equal today's cost of survival.

With some encouraging exceptions, one party goes way too fast in the wrong direction and the other party goes way too slow in the right one.

At the beginning of year 2021, to take inflation into account, the actual minimum hourly wage survival level for a family of four would need to be $21.50 (per CNBC). In fact the Congressional struggle is from the present $7.25 to be changed to $15 (but still no cost-of-living annual adjustment) with the oppositional party wanting less or zero. Even more considerate politicians remind me of what was said about former president Richard Nixon:

*"If somebody is drowning 100 feet off shore, he'll throw them 50 feet of rope and say 'Hey! I met you half way!' "*

The argument against any improvement says jobs will be lost even though millions of people may be raised above the poverty level. The business often stated in this discussion is a small business struggling itself to survive and unable to pay workers more. I think of Albuquerque's unique Tunisian *Kasbah* restaurant run by Ridha Bouajila or the *Chillz* original frozen custard concoctions designed, made, and served by Justin Carson. Santa Fe and just about any town in New Mexico can match this.

Where are they now? Originality plus a year of pandemic quarantine couldn't save most of them. A few survived and a few more will emerge. We should care. We should help. Patronize the best of them in large numbers. Tip generously. It's our state's culinary art.

Some states, like ours, may reduce costs for the small independents, including the minimum wage. Still a challenge for the wait staff though.

But: look closer. A "*small* business" is defined by our government as less than *500* workers. In fact, the average small business has only ten. Are we ignoring the impact of ever-growing for-profit corporations in this debate? And almost half the Americans working today are underpaid (CBS news).

Back to the wait staff. Oh they were not allowed to be included in the minimum wage level other American workers get. The servers get only $2.13 (!) an hour in most states. Unless, in some other states, tips are said to equal the $7.25 other workers get. Confusing? Not much to live on in any state.

In New Mexico, with the present state government, it improved as of January 2021 to an hourly minimum wage of $10.50 with wait staff raised to $6.30 plus enough tips to raise wages to the $10.50 minimum like everybody else. Many restaurants pay better and bless them. But: survival level?

What about the big chains, owned in turn by corporations or investment entities? Ones well able to pay real survival wages. But don't. Big enough to avoid many taxes. Big enough to innovate cost-cutting. One of the most profitable of these was shorting the restaurant servers. And the customers. And the taxpayers.

Tips are an optional gift, and should not be a server's taxable income. The difference between the $2.13/hour, depending on the state, and the minimum wage of that state is now being paid by the tips. From us. Shifting the burden of an almost survival wage to the customer. And, since survival is still not paid for, government steps in with SNAP (food stamps) and other almost survival nets which will save the big chains wage costs. Subsidized by taxpayers. By us again.

Fifty feet of rope. Going under the tide at 100 feet.

How do wait staff cope? Many jobs, long shifts, sleep in car? There are websites to blow off steam if not to buy groceries. "*WELP*" is a newer one that allows ratings of customers by wait staff. Others like *waiters-revenge.com* exist to share various traumas, some with humor. Spitting in food would/should risk the job. And yes, pandemic issues in mind, few wait staff have a job for now with indoor dining service at even minimum wage.

But restaurants are coming back, some already, probably all the rest in this calendar year. Tips are now more often expected at the 20% level when service is decent. Survival? We can do better. Much better. Those elected by us in the Roundhouse can do better too. As can the United States Congress. How about having a minimum wage that applies to ALL working people? No more excluding workers that *might* get tips. Tipping is optional. Tips *are* gifts, *not* income. No matter how good the service, some wait staff are rarely tipped, especially in economically depressed neighborhoods. Some customers can't *afford* to tip. Waitresses and waiters deserve the same minimum wage safety net that others get. And one at a fair survivable level. Also: let's not forget the need for a cost-of-living annual adjustment. Save the politicians some debating time.

So: when one of our elected representatives, state or national, *opposes* fair survival compensation for working

Americans, remember the optionally tipped workers. Visit that politician in person if you can.

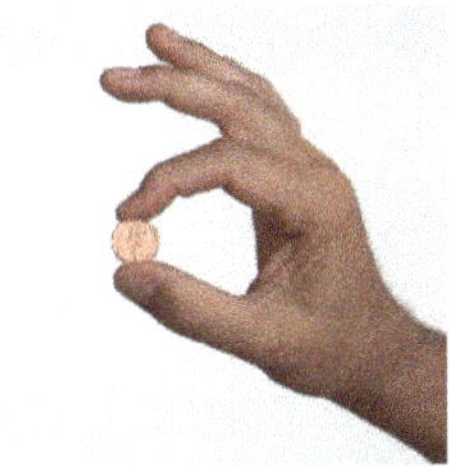

Then tip them a penny.

*This far into the 21st Century, time to move past reruns, sequels, and prequels to do more theater that fits today's challenges in our daily life.*

***GRATUITY, THE MUSICAL***

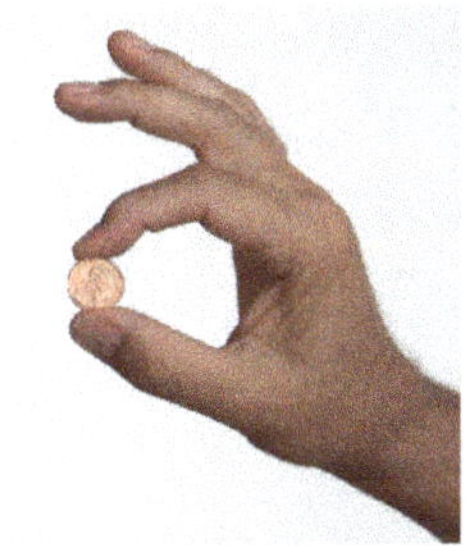

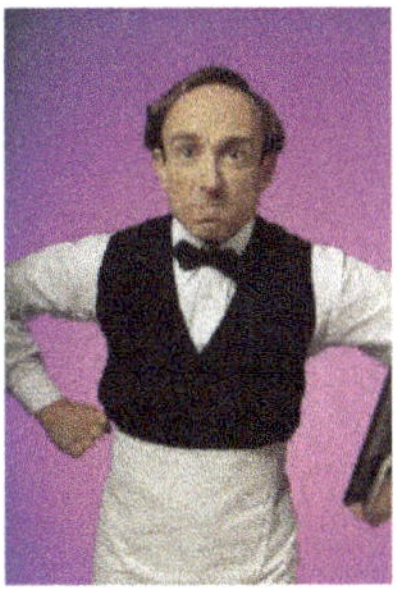

**SONGS** (partial list)

***Miss! You forgot your penny!***

***Below Minimum***

***Tipping Saint Peter***

***Two is an army***

***Onerous Owners***

***Ain't No Sunshine When You're Here Neither***

***2 wrongs don't make a right but 3 do***

***The Singapore Solution***

***A Higher Power***

***Thank you for your service***

**Story** Two women meet when one of them is chased for blocks by an irate waiter who she had tipped a penny for bad service. They look into the sad practice of paying restaurant servers below minimum wage with customers expected to fix this owner inequity by tipping. They take up for restaurant workers, learning of many bad ways to help them, the "counter revolution" included, and find in the end legislative hope. Fun doing all this. *(Casting Suggestion: Bring Angel Morgan and Audra McDonald together again 40 years since their high school's "Anything Goes" musical.)*

# The Curve's Frontier

**Theme**: *Soul Sacrifice* Santana

## The Normal Curve

There are many cases where what we are measuring or counting tends to be around a central value with no pile-up left or right. It's called a "Normal Distribution" like this:

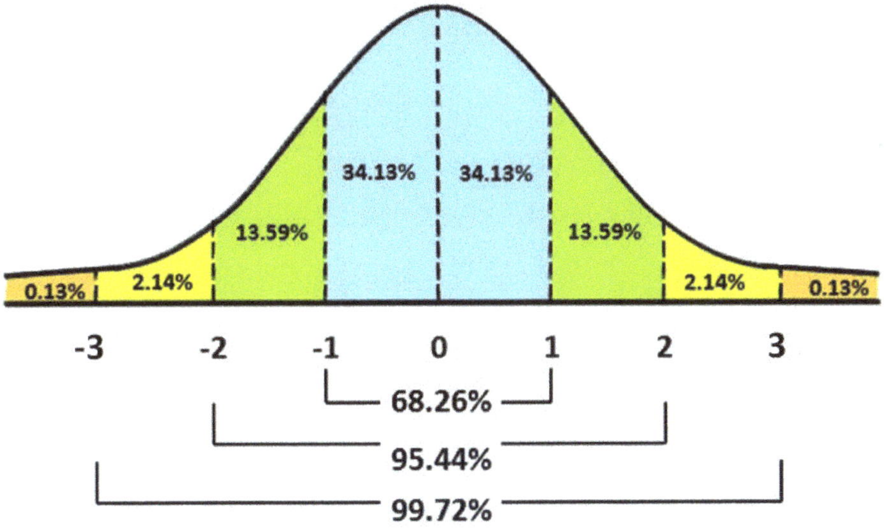


It is sometimes called a "Bell Curve" because it looks like a bell.

Many things closely follow a Normal Distribution: heights of people, size of eggs, factory products, blood pressure, IQ, test grades, blue collar salaries, core body temperature.

Also a human ability or disability. Sometimes one is mistaken for the other.

Then too, a full range of any population's body age can fit the normal curve. We do grow old at different individual rates. For any of these distributions, you find the rarest cases at the extreme opposite edges of the distribution.

These can be a tiny fraction of 1% (0.13% in diagram on the previous page.).

## Progeria

Progeria is a rare event. No more common than one in four million or more births.

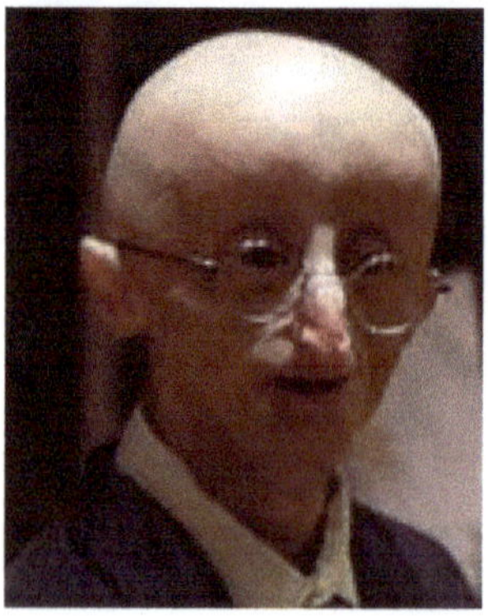

These babies age very fast physically with a lifespan usually under 20. Mentally and emotionally they usually do advance normally.

Such an extremely mature and thoughtful person was Sam Berns who lived to 17 the year of this photo.

Then came *Kimberly Akimbo,* winning the 2023 Best Musical Tony award for the story of a girl with progeria facing her demise with resigned but joyful and melodious beauty.

An elegant way to let the public know about this rare terminal condition. One not often experienced with melodious joy.

Where does it come from? Multiple causality: lots of suspects. Genetics research hot on one trail. Medical Treatment? Not yet.

## Syndrome X

Some babies don't seem to grow older as years go by. There can be several medical causes for this but in a few rare cases none of them seem to apply. Without a known medical diagnosis, it has been called Syndrome X.

Brooke Greenberg was one such baby. In her case, she did not progress physically and was only slowly maturing mentally. Learning occurred but still left her acting and looking like a baby even though her teen years.

Here she is 16 years old:

From the outset she was tested and retested for every known malady that might have caused her condition.

Still seeing this as a disease, interventions were tried. Without success.

Like the Progerian Sam Berns, she too had loving and caring parents, ones providing impressive concentrations of valuable time.

Despite all of this, she died at the age of twenty.

Her father, in a television interview, suggested that future research, especially genetics, might find ways to slow the normal aging process for all of us, especially the ones leading to deterioration and death.

I think he was right.

In that way, the short lives of these loved and impressive children may have an extra contribution to make.

Meantime, of course, they will always continue to exist in their time and place.

Statues in time, definitely high art.

## The Curve's Frontier

There continue to be more babies born with Progeria or Syndrome X.

If we step out of the medical perspective, we can see them as at opposite extremes of the normal human aging range. Most of us die in a very close cluster of chronological age.

Yet doesn't it stand to reason that a very few have much longer or lesser lifespans than our average group? Not a disease but a distribution. Therein is the Curve's edge frontier.

Genetics may be a key to this, much as it dominates height, weight, eye color. So certainly genetics can be impacted by environment. It can be modified or redirected as research progresses.

This then makes it a genuine frontier of the future.

On the other hand, to the extent no damaging or lethal symptoms are found, no disease identified, maybe we should just leave the healthy babies to grow into their rare long lifespan unmolested by elective surgery, “heroic” or high risk interventions, or hazardous diagnostic methods.

Excessive Xray scans, operations, stressful ICUs, multiple side effects, all might bring about iatrogenic (medical mistake) damage to vulnerable Syndrome X babies. Per Heisenberg, measuring changes what’s being measured. Often in not a good way.

For some of these babies, there may be no real emergency. No crisis.

Just a *very* long life if we don’t shorten it.

Something to consider.

# Deep Obedience

**Themes:** *I Still Believe* Tim Cappello; *You've Got to be Carefully Taught (South Pacific)* Rodgers &

Hammerstein, Mandy Patinkin, James Taylor; *Anytime* Ray Charles, Patsy Cline, Eddy Arnold

*When a charismatic cult leader or politician says something obviously untrue, followers may conform and pretend it is true. Yet a growing group of followers will, in their own minds, actually believe the new opposite of their former reality. They live in the perceptual world that their leader ordained for them. A break from consensual reality. This trickle-down psychosis can be called "deep obedience". That is not new in human history. Though it is a growing cancer in the first quarter of the 21st century.*

*There can be immunity. Ask Maddy.*

## Maddy

*This story is true. Only Maddy's name is not.*

Her birth certificate name was "*Mademoiselle Gray*" just as her parents had decided. So of course she was called "*Maddy*" for the rest of her life.

More people could spell it.

Maddy lived in a rough Detroit setting. It was decades ago in the late middle of the 20th century.

Her teenage girl friends often became pregnant as soon as it was physically possible. Maddy's mother decided to send her daughter to a residential Catholic Convent girl's school for her final years of high school, ages 13-18.

Reluctantly but obediently, Maddy complied.

## The School

The academics were competent but the greatest emphasis was on rules and rewards.

RULE # 1: **Thought obedience.**

**The class exercises in thought obedience went like this.**

**The teacher held up a colored piece of paper. If it was blue, the girls were told to look at it until it became the color their teacher said it was; until the Blue became Red because they were told so.**

**Just the molding of young minds.**

RULE #2: Erotic pairing denial.

The girls were told they must never be alone with another girl or great punishment would follow.

This puzzled Maddy and her friends, not understanding the frustrated sexual projections of the nuns. Good behavior did have unusual rewards at the end of each week.

The top two rewards for good behavior:

REWARD # 1: One hour alone with another girl.

REWARD # 2: One hour standing by the west wall of the convent at a specific time and day. When this was accomplished, the girl could hear the marching by of the boys from the military academy on the other side of the wall. And have an orgasm.

Most became very well behaved when with their teachers. They had adapted, learned to see the world exactly as they were told to see it. **Blue** turned **Red** when described as such. Alternative facts became the true facts.

Though, so far, this compliance only extended to the convent school nuns.

Back at home was another matter.

## Consequences

All the girls came home for holidays in November.

For Christmas they returned to home a second time.

Many by now were clearly pregnant from their first visit.

## Immunization

Maddy's mother was quick to reverse her mistake. Her daughter was re-enrolled in a public school where she soon excelled. Her fine mind and careful skepticism for authority was fully restored.

Maddy went on in life to be a top administrator at a major university.

At the Convent Girl's School, Maddy had never fully allowed the nuns to make her mind see **Red** when the paper was **Blue**. Her teenage rebellion served her well here.

She, in the freedom of her own mind, saw **Blue** as **Blue**.

This path for sanity is our way forward too.

## The Song

Maddy liked to rewrite the lyrics of songs to support her independence, her freedom of thought.

While at the school, she had in her mind aimed this secret one at her teachers: ***"Anytime***

*Anytime you're feeling lonely*

*Anytime you're feeling **Blue***

*That's the time to remember*

*That OUR troubles come from YOU."*

As a mature woman, she kept the song in her thoughts.

But she revised her personal lyric to remind herself that she was now responsible, free, for her own life.

And had the determination to stand up to anybody demanding deep belief.

Now it had become:

"***Anytime***

*Anytime I'm feeling lonely*

*Anytime you're feeling* ***Blue***

*That's the time to remember*

*That YOUR troubles come from YOU."*

## The Trickle-Down Psychosis

Here in the 21st century we are regularly confronted with "*alternative facts*" proclaimed by a leader of deep believers. A world view asserting the opposite of the truth, a break with reality. A trickle-down psychosis.

Deep believers comply perceptually with the will of that leader.

Deeply loyal beyond belief.

Literally.

Familiar?

-

Rollo May told me that *"PESSIMISM and OPTIMISM are classic mistakes. The word I believe in is HOPE."*

I agree. What word comes best after "HOPE"?

We each live in a finite lifespan. Eventually our residence in temporal space will come to an end.

Knowing this, we are challenged to appreciate what we have, a statue in time. Living it fully, a day at a time.

The key to our best future, all of us.

This next word we choose, as you would surely approve Rollo, is "JOY".

The ancients had a god for this: Dionysus, the God of Joy.

And theater.

Maybe some of these ancient Greeks understood that each one of their days had value.

Not then always in an ethical or compassionate manner.

Nor can we find these positive values reliably in our 21st century either.

Still, may you find your best JOY in this and every day you have yet to come.

# Future Time Statues

Time is a place. Each moment is a statue in time, always rooted in that time and that place. In this book's lifespan revisits to international time statues from the first quarter of the 21st century, they are followed by ones in the rest of the century that might come after. Or not. Here they are.

# The Cheese Contest

**Theme**: *Cheese Shop Song* Monty Python

The newspaper was bunched up on the floor. A read only well known to university inhabitants- *The Chronicle of Higher Education*. I wasn't going to pick it up until I saw the intriguing headline ***THE CHEESE CONTEST.***

Turned out that a major cheese company had promised a very rich prize to any college department winning a contest for creative new uses for, of all things, cheese.

Now heading my department was no big deal and that's the way I liked it. Finally settling down to the teaching I love while managing a very small number of bright cantankerous individual faculty. Time to think, time to enjoy the days, even look forward to each one.

But we were under-resourced. The tuition money flowed in and where it went was an ongoing debate. Clearly it had not gone much beyond subsistence to us.

Until now?

Well, I brought it up to the dozen faculty I supervised at our next meeting. Laughter, growls. But then I mentioned the generous prize. For the fun of it, I challenged them to try it.

Madeline stepped forward, claimed we could win this if only she could pick her own equally gifted, almost, senior faculty as a working group.

I nodded and she picked three other faculty for her posse. Left right away with them.

I suggested the remaining folks develop any submission on their own. Agreed.

We set a week later to turn in all our submissions as a package from me and our department. Madeline's posse also accepted that deadline.

## The Group

On deadline day, all submissions were in, a promptness feat never before or after equaled by these faculty.

Madeline's group effort produced a very scholarly submission, complete with references, citations, footnotes. It briefly discussed the origin of cheese, the cultural disdain for it, like in Japan, and the key debates. For creative new uses, they outlined research approaches not yet attempted.

It was a comprehensive and academically impressive document.

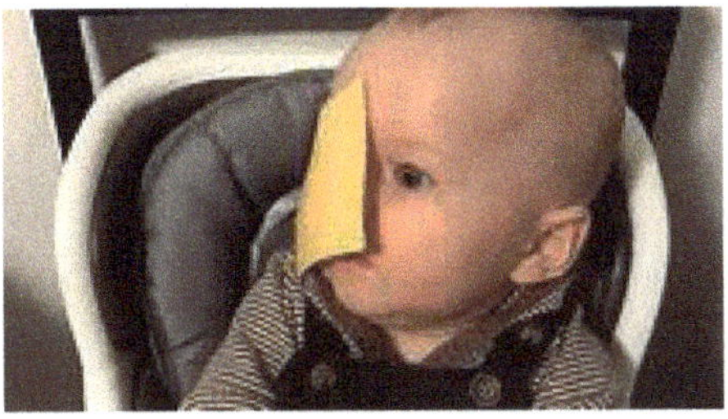
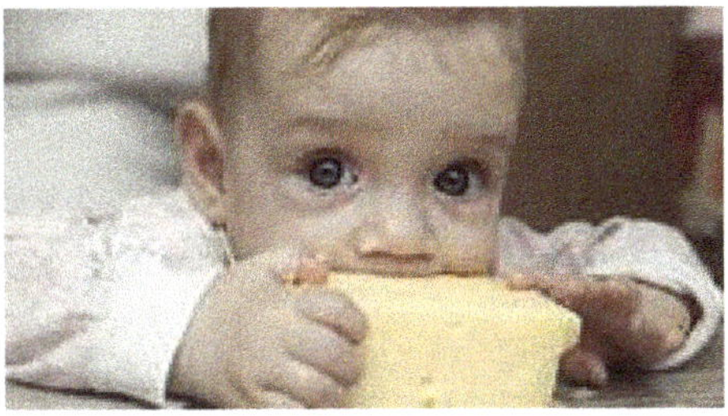

So, of course, impossible to win.

I sent it in anyway.

## The Individuals

Eight individual tries sat on my desk for review. I added my own as the ninth.

Each one was brief, creative, original, and had a shot.

One of the older faculty, Mervin, just had fun with it.

He was habitually skeptical of everything.

**Hard Cheese**- For an innovation with cheese, Mervin designed a block of it as a doorstop.

The others were each more creative.

**Health Blend-** One suggested mixing in fruit juice to cheddar, adding color and flavor.

Maybe wheat grass too. Uppers as needed for energy.

**Final Fragrance**- One promoted the West-meets-East idea of adding Durian to Limburger so as to expand the overwhelming stink and despair.

Or an alternative idea where a deliberate massive cheese overdose in tiny micro-dose form could be used where legal for cheese-assisted suicide.

**Thanksgiving** -One wanted cheese converted to a liquid gravy to go with cheese powdered stuffing. Or using the cheese powder as makeup or deodorant.

**Calendar Daily Edible**. One wanted it in an edible calendar form, including a different cheese for each month, a taste for every day.

Also a liquefied baked-bean-saturated cheese stick for selected flatulence usage.

**Cheese Bliss**- Another submission promoted cheese as a vehicle for enhancing sexual pleasure with various blended ingredients. Cheese as a marijuana edible was optional.

**Burger-less Cheeseburgers**. I did wonder at this idea of enhancing beef flavoring in cheese so as to have a cheeseburger without the burger.

Or adding any other flesh product flavor (Vegan faculty person)..

**Holy Holes**- Another alternative promised on-the-cheese facial images of holy deities, one each to each variety of cheese. She also added the option for those acquiring more cheese than they could eat, the holes grew larger with time until all cheese was gone.

For my part:

**Cheese Gelato**-Blending cheese with gelato seemed strange enough not to have been tried before. So too were the suggested cheese cones.

And also, deference to my brother's early book *Talking Chips.*:

**Talking Cheese**- One added edible talking chips to a variety of popular cheeses so as to make them more orally seductive. Sighs as needed

I sent them all in as our department submissions.

And learned that my faculty did much better on their own than in a group.

## The Prize Winner

Mervin's father had been a chemist.

Using what he had learned from him, Mervin had made his cheese doorstop impossible to penetrate or destroy.

His ingredients were far less expensive than anything going into steel or armor.

He quickly patented his mix, becoming a very rich man in all of his many elder years to come.

Not too cheesy.

# Mausoleum with a Doorbell

**Theme:** *Time Will Tell* Susan Anton

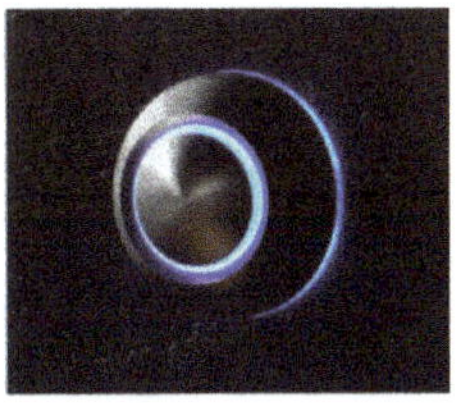

*Do not go gentle into that good night,*
*Old age should burn and rave at close of day;*
*Rage, rage against the dying of the light.*
–Dylan Thomas

As a child in my 4th year of life I loved to read the stories and poems by the Scottish writer Robert Louis Stevenson, Treasure Island especially. I then read of his final years on Samoa. Then there were no televisions or internet or movies or even radio. The key modality of entertainment and tradition was only story telling. Stevenson excelled at this. Soon he was surrounded by Samoans of all ages, eagerly awaiting more of his adventures. They named him Tusitala or the teller of stories. He had finally found his best audience, a writer's dream. When he died suddenly of a stroke at the young age of 44, the epitaph he had written for such an occasion was engraved on his tomb, there in Samoa:

**Under the wide and starry sky,**

**Dig the grave and let me lie.**

**Glad did I live and gladly die,**

**And I laid me down with a will.**

**This be the verse you grave for me:**

**Here he lies where he longed to be;**

**Home is the sailor, home from sea,**

**And the hunter home from the hill.**

Reading of this at that tender age, I thought I wanted to spend my own final days, my life in the last lane, producing stories to such a very wonderful audience. I took eight decades to realize that this was a purpose in life I had been looking for.

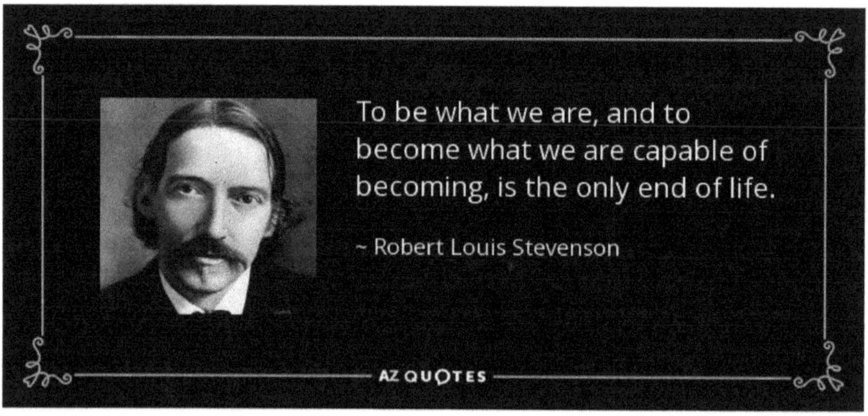


## King Henosis

Last night I had this dream.

I was somebody in Ancient Greece. The competition between the wealthy was intense: who would be acclaimed as the best hosts. The measure of success was what welcome guests would say on exit. Hot baths, gentle masseuses, fine food and wines, unforgettable beds.

That last led many to whisper about Procrustes, as few left his estate with any complaints. Some never left at all. The rumor was, for example, that any guest complaining to Procrustes that their bed was too short would have their feet cut off until they fit. Complaint about a bed too long would get them stretched on a torture rack until *they* better fit. Procrustes denied all this. But soon his name would describe excessive pressure for conformity, as "*Procrustean*" does even today.

The entertainment there and then centered on the retelling of grand stories, especially those begun by blind Homer (not the Simpsons one) about the long war between Troy (Turkey today) and the Greek kings of city states, not to omit interventions by the Gods on both sides (Gods possibly based on a high mountain culture of more advanced warriors than the smaller Greeks.)

One shorter new story was about a young king from generations before. As kings go, he was one of the better ones. Sure, he expected obedience, though not in a destructive Procrustean way. And he got it. His people felt safe in their high altitude home, hard for strangers to find. The king himself used their apparent safety to encourage the arts, creative expression, probing ideas, deep appreciation of nature, of life. He was a philosopher king. His people were happier than most in that era of temporal geography.

They had some sentries and soldiers but not enough by far. Another king, simply eager to take from others, found a way for his army to get to them. The battle was fierce even so but in the end the invading soldiers won.

The good king was bound to his throne, now moved outside. The invading king sat freely in another throne, elevated on a hill overlooking the captive king. All those surviving the battle gathered to watch.

The invader king motioned to what looked like a parade to march between the two thrones. The first to pass held the severed head of the good king's wife. He saw this but sat upright with no expression on his face. Those closest saw his muscles clench but clearly he was not about to give the invader king any satisfaction. Next came a procession of the invading soldiers, each waving the severed head of the good king's children. Again no response from the bound king. The crowd was increasingly impressed by his resolve, his iron strength in the face of such tragedy. Next came the heads of his closest friends. Still no response as he suppressed his grief with great will.

Lastly, lagging behind the bloody parade, came a giant invader soldier holding the severed head of the bound king's dog. It was barely past puppyhood and still beautiful even in this setting of horror. At this last, the king's resolve ended and he sobbed loudly.

On hearing this story, the Greek audience debated whether the king cried for the pet because he cared more for it than all the rest, or whether it was just the final hurt to release the whole suppressed anguish for all the decapitated victims. No resolution of this debate expected, they did decide on a name for the good royal: King Henosis.

I was in the body of an elder Greek named for Henosis. My Henosis was a famous actor though most felt was well past his prime. Still, this Henosis had resources and launched a Greek Tragedy for the stage to replay this sad story from their distant past. Further, he insisted on playing the young king, despite his older age. It was to be the peak of his acting career. And so it was.

There on the stage I sat bound to a throne, as now I am the aged actor. I reached the point of explosive grief at last. Drawing on all the pain and disappointment of my life, I sobbed loud enough to reach every Greek in that audience. In the midst of this theatrical triumph, a woman's voice came from the sky: "*Wake up! Everything is okay now!*" A goddess? Interrupting my acting scene's triumph?

No. My wife, being a helpful dream catcher. And so I woke.

Clearly, the aged Greek actor in the dream was me, a writer in his 80s revisiting the time statues of his life. Even the painful ones. Living them in stories as on a stage. But the rest? King Henosis?

The next morning I learned that the name "*Henosis*" was what the ancient Greeks called seeing the essence of things, a unity with nature, with the universe. Some, who have had a stroke impacting logical Procrustean left brain activity, or have had training to pause left brain activity, then may experience a right brain experience that becomes one with all the family of life. In this way our language has kept King Henosis living on as a guide to us.

Beyond local space and time, send him thanks and comfort when he needed it most.

I had no idea I would meet him in person and soon.

# Leadville

**Theme:** *The Mountains High* (Dick and Dee Dee)

Leadville, Colorado, is the highest incorporated town in America. In the 19th century it was the most populated city in the state after Denver. Doc Holliday had his last job as the law there then.

Mining, especially silver, brought people there and to a slightly lower neighboring town three miles away in a town named Climax. They've heard all the jokes.

Even today tourists still go to Leadville. From Denver, already a mile high, they drive a few hours uphill to Salida, a name meaning "*exit*", and truly depart any 'flatlander' geography as they drive ever higher, past Climax, to enter Lake County and finally Leadville.

Of course, most of the year the cold weather centered on Leadville might block this trip. Crisp snow then hugs the city. Or did, but the global warming behind climate change may yet make Leadville a great place to be.

For now, our tourists arrive in the summer. Still cooler than most places, refreshing. Just don't stay in the sun for long. The UV rays at that altitude can burn you quickly. Too much exposure, for some only minutes, could be dangerous, lethal.

Let's assume these tourists are young and athletic. They don't worry about the sun. With full confidence they look for residents to show off their visitor skills. Not hard to find some senior citizen residents to challenge in a run or for a tennis match.

The seniors are used to the thin air at that elevation, the young tourists are not. The tourists lose any contest quickly to the seniors, very soon running out of breath.

Maybe a visiting Sherpa could do better but not many others. That's why race horses aren't allowed to compete if raised at high elevation. Mountain animals or people experience sea level as walking in soupy air, excessive oxygen. Their stronger lungs, greater strength, supplies a huge advantage. Flatlanders used to swimming in abundantly thick air have altitude weakness or even sickness on the mountains.

Still, the view here is great. Even better, at more than 10,000 feet above sea level, you can still see peaks 4,000 feet higher.

Leadville is as far as tourists usually go, but if we actually travel to one of those peaks, we can find a small town nestled in the protective embrace of two mountains.

The people are friendly, having very few visitors, so, after a rest and a great meal, one takes us to what they think we came to see. They are right.

## Introductions

Our guide is the Mayor. I'm a semi-retired clinical psychologist. Today, I'm just a tourist on a vacation trip. Sort of.

My companion is a past client of my psychotherapy practice. Let's call him 'Andrew' since that's what his parents did.

In Andrew's last visit he thanked me for a successful intervention and used the confidentiality of the meeting to share the existence of this place. He knew I would keep they key town name, and exact directions there secret if I said I would. I did so.

He also wanted me to experience something wonderful there as a thank you.

Finally, he told me it would be okay to share some of this trip with the world in my writing if I chose.

So, as we walk, I quietly record these thoughts.

Another introduction of an individual will be forthcoming soon.

If Andrew is right.

## Cemetary

The town cemetary is just ahead.

But first we must walk through a forest path to get there.

Maybe another photo will help.

Trees are living beings.

I no longer pluck their leaves while on our way.

This way. On this path.

I thank them, wish them well.

Moving on, I recall that live-in milkman, Bob, stepping out on our Nova Scotia home's balcony each night to address any audience (or none).

Quoting always the same Robet Frost poem:

*"The woods are lovely, dark and deep. But I have promises to keep, and miles to go before I sleep."*

And sleep then he would.

Almost there now, says Andrew.

Once the ghost sun is all but gone, the transition to moonlight has changed the color of the forest'

Somwhat misty now. Hard to focus. The sun is setting.

The forest light is suddenly amazing.

This is the ghost moment for the sun.

The actual sun has set but light takes a little time to show us that.

The interim here in this moment is dramatic.

Worth another photo

And now we come to more hidden cemetary.

As we enter, I stow the camera on my phone.

There is a lone building overlooking this cemetary.

On a hill with a set of stairs.

We take the stairs.

At the top we see that the building is a mausoleum.

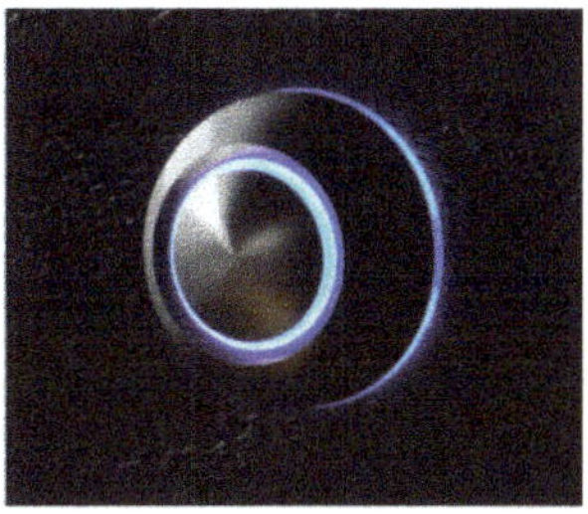

It has a doorbell.

Which is glowing.

Andrew rings the doorbell.

## Henosis

The heavy door slowly swings open.

A very tall man, powerfully built, with long hair.

He stands in the doorway.

Looks to be in his late twenties but he seems much older.

He gestures us to enter. We do.

We follow him down a long staircase with guard rails. Clearly far underground by a long shot. Temperature comfortable.

Into a well lit antechamber with comfortable chairs. That light just seems to radiate from the walls.

Behind us and further down is what looks like a large theater or meeting place, maybe more after that.

He sits facing us and we sit as well, finding the chairs comfortable, reassuring.

Andrew was silent looking very respectful. Then he turned to me. Said quietly that we would now make our contribution.

Our host speaks. "*Call me Luke. I know Andrew of course and, with your permission, I would like to know you.*"

I nodded yes and meant to speak. But was swallowed in a warm black cloud,

I woke, not sure how much time had passed. I felt rested, centered, safe.

Luke said "*Welcome back. It was only minutes. So now I know you.*"

It should have been concerning but at the time it made sense. Besides I was floating, content, a little tired as one feels after exercise.

He went on. "*I trust you now. I can answer your questions fully, as much as I understand them.*"

He smiled and though I had asked no questions, he seemed to know them all.

In fact this began the most incredible dialogue of my life. I never spoke but he each time received the question I thought to ask him. And his answers! The words were given along with visual wrap-arounds- we were there experientially in whatever he was recalling.

Luke continued. "*I was very touched by your compassion for me on the day of my death and transformation. Back in my last torturous human moments of life as what you call King Hemosis.*"

He paused, giving me time to aborb this. Andrew sat enthralled. So: safe.

Luke, seeing me smile and nod (I was in such an unexpectedly mellow mood!) went on with his explanation. Along with the visual around us.

*"The story, for all its millenia of duration, is not far off the mark of reality. We, my people and me, lived on top of a famous Greek mountain. Most of those tribes living below us thought of us as gods. Since we were larger, lived longer, and had discovered more."*

*"But this fascination led them to spy on us continually, take sides in our disputes, thank us or blame us for things we had nothing to do with. Much of their gossip eventually emerged in a blind Greek poet's stories. Oral histories well distorted. Mixed in with an ancient battle between what are now called Turks and Greeks."*

# The Snake People

**Theme:** *Snake Farm* Ray Wylie Hubbard

*"But at the time just before my own battle, my brother had established his own small kingdom. Snake worshippers. It was not far below us. They envied our greater success. Some of what you might call giants, survivors from Mars (yes, they too had a mass extinction). With the assistance of these large allies, they invaded."*

*"Actually, we repelled them. Not once but many times. I was urged to carry the battle to them and end it. No, I wnted family peace. A mistake. In the end they won. With our own surviving people watching from a distance, they did execute my family in front of me. Including my life-long wolf companion. I was overwhelmed. My heart was shutting down. I knew I was seconds away from death. "*

Here Luke paused to hand me a photo copy. "*This is a small descendant of my wolf, what you now call dogs. His heart had stopped after being hit by a car. One of Andrew's daughters brought his body to me, hoping I could help. Well, the little one had not been dead for long so he was easy for me to revive. The girl told me her animal friend was named Arnold, took this pacture of us."*

*"Yes, you can keep the photo. Use it as you will. Privacy matters little now as our own mass extinction has begun its middle phase."*

I naturally wanted to know more about this mass extinction phase. But Luke decided to come back to his history lesson. So this is the photograph he gave me.

Luke continued: "*The oral history that you knew ends too soon. Actually, confronted by my brother and all his soldiers, smirking over the bodies of my innocent family, I felt overcome with rage. Though I was tied tightly to my throne, the bonds fell away. Yet I could not move. My own body was limp, left behind, as my spirit rushed these killers in a tsunami wave of energy. The wave swallowed their energy- I know no other way to describe it. They, every one, fell to ashes.*"

" "*It was too late to save my family. My energy wave, magnified by what I had absorbed from the invaders, returned to my now dead body. Entered and revived me as something else.*"

"*My heart and lungs then functioned as did my brain but all were powered by this energy wave, further magnified by the energy taken from the invaders. In time I realized that this was my food. No longer did I care about ingestion, digestion, excretion, or normal physical processes of human life.*"

"*I rose from the throne, radiating new life. Stepped forward. But my own people, watching this from a higher point, ran. Terrified.*"

"*Yes, I was called a vampire or worse. But blood was not needed. Over time I learned to absorb small amounts of energy from volunteers in exchange for answering questions or otherwise helping.*"

*"Where did I go? I wandered down past the flatlanders and eventually to the ocean. You wouldn't know this of mountain people but we were born in water. My own mother had me in a water birth. We always loved to swim. So I joined the dolphins for a lifetime or so."*

*"Dolphins are a higher lifeform. Playful. Yet with larger more advanced brains. By mutual consent dolphins can share direct experience- to be in the world through each other's senses. A version of which I am doing with you now. And their spoken language! Fast high pitched concentrations of so much, stories, feelings, music. I learned so much from them! In the end though, I went on back to the human world."*

*"Where? The next stop was Egypt. Such advanced chemical and biological science, farther along than is found today. Their morality not so much- slavery, autocracy, war. Genetic experiments blending animal DNA into people. Tragic. A few of these mixes did survive and were worshipped. They were not happy. And then the visitors that came from ... Another story. I digress. I did keep wandering, creating a presence in generation after generation, always wandering.*

*"Oh. I see your other questions are accumulating. Thank you for your restraint. I will asnwer some more now."*

*"Oh no, I don't miss the taste of food. With the consent of my enrgy donors, I also retain certain gift memories,*

*especially wonderful food tastes among them. I only share what is given freely but my guests are quite generous."*

*"Another question? No, you don't need to speak them out loud. You have a strong mind. Infact your questions are quite loud as I receive them."*

*"Mass extinction? Oh you know about that. The euphamism is 'climate change' or even 'global warming'. It is caused by human greed of the wealthiest. Its termed by scientists as the 'Anthropocene", a human-caused mass extinction, well under way."*

*"Oh. What can I do to help? Not much at this point. Though I do love the story told about Saint Francis walking on the beach with a friend and seeing thousands of little sea creatures washed up to die there on land. Francis began tossing some back to ocean survival, one at a time. His friend told him that what he was doing wouldn't matter since there were thousands more breathing their last on the sand than any one person could throw back. Francis held up another one and said 'It matters to this one', tossing the lucky survivor back into the ocean. I'm no Saint Francis but I can at least save the people of this town and even those in Leadville."*

*"Many decades ago, I bought this hill and the Mausoleum on it. With a view of a cemetary and considering the climate, the purchase was a bargain. It included all the land below which, turns out, is an extensive mountain with*

*caves, air pockets, and an underground stream of water. Goes on for miles."*

*"So under this hill, work is continually extending living quarters large enough for the survival of those living in this region. Underground is a constant room temperature.At this elevation and in this within-mountain home, we should be free from the flood and fire. At least for a generation or several. Does it matter? Yes, it does to them. And to me."*

*"I did of course put in a doorbell so local visitors could come by. When I am open to such visits it will glow as it did today for you and Andrew."*

*"What powers that I have discovered that might help? Well, there is my form of time travel."*

*"Yes, travel in time. Within yourself. I see that in your clinical practice you once had a patient who trusted nobody, not even you, but desperatelly needed advice for some essential life choices. Through hypnosis you connected her to an older version of herself. In this way she gave herself good advice and best choices were made."*

*" You also are aware of, umm, the theory of your good friend William Braud that healing the adult of trauma can ripple back in time to healing that adult as a child. Thinking of things in that way can lead you to time travel."*

*"Through meditation, hypnosis, safe hallucinogen substances, other ways, one can go back in time to your-*

*self at a younger age. Look through their eyes, assist them in key choices. Yes, I have done this. Yes, my own unique energy state makes it easier. But I do think that living humans can learn to do this."*

*"Have I done it? Yes. I did assist some later Hebrew tribes write a portion of their history scrolls. Its where I got the name Luke from."*

*"Why don't I go back to my younger self as King Henosis and save my family? Ah, I wish! But then I would never have transformed, so a paradox. I've tried but I keep being snapped gack to the present."*

*"Yes, a past without the paradox can be diverted or improved but one needs to be very cautious. Do these statues in tme change for the better? If not, are we just creating a different multiverse? Maybe worse?"*

*" Oh! Yes, I see you tried this travel back to a younger self in the 1970s. Just visual though. Seeing yourself in the mirror at a younger age. Hmm. True, now you look into a mirror wondering if an older self is looking back (laughter). Creepy huh?"*

*"Have I left anything out of my own history that I would like to tell you? What a kind question! Let me consider this."*

*"Well, yes. As I've shown you, my people who had seen me destroy my brother and his troops were so frightened of me*

*that I had to leave them to wander my own path about the earth. So many lives."*

*"The descendants of my brother's family, from those that had not invaded, eventually told a lie to the Greek and Hebrew tribes. A version stolen from the story of the Romulus and Remus brothers."*

*"Said that since I had killed my own brother, I had been condemned by Zeus (and his son Jezeus) to wander the earth forever. Made people hate me as well as fear. My brother was the aggressor, not me."*

*"The Hebrew tribes paid me a tribute by placing a tribal mark on my arm. The lie from mmy brother's descendants claimed it was a mark of divine condemnation for his death. Not to long ago I covered it over with a tatoo better expressing my truth."*

Luke handed me another photo, this time of his tattoo:

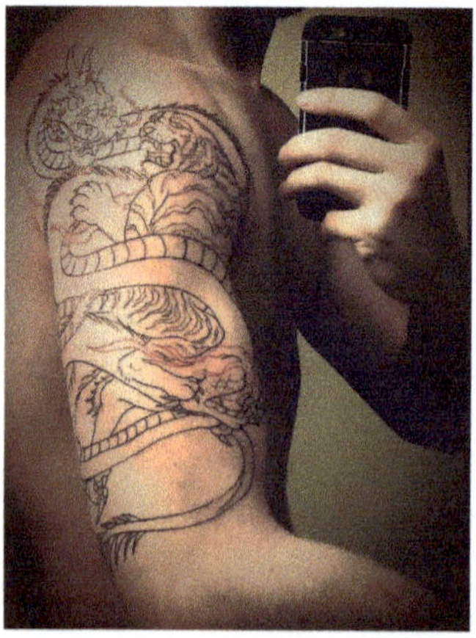

*"It combines the dragon and tiger branches of my existence. Indigenous myths in what is now called England refer to Arthur as a Pendragon or son of a dragon."*

*"A Romanian saga remembers its king as a dragon or "Dracul" in that language. His more famous*

*son is simularly referred to as the son of this dragon or, in Romanian, "Dracula".*

*"The tiger represents my Chinese family line and a more admirable brother there."*

*" Yes, I may have been more involved in all of these during my own wanderings. How I might have been involved .. anther day, another conversation. "*

*"For now, we can see the dragon and tiger eclipsing that prior mark I carried for far too long. One so misunderstood. Good riddance."*

*"Finally, I also took my brother's name from those Hebrew and Christian tribe's unjust myth about me. Giving me that hostile name, a target for the world. So I took that brother's ancient name as my own last name. Just to further defuse the issue."*

*" With that substitution, my name is now officially 'Luke Abel'. Maybe an extra 'L'?"*

*" Anyway, never again will I be called 'Cain'."*

-

**Note:** This was the first of four stories excerpted from *Time Statue Dreams* with permission. Thanks are added here for Luke Abell, my grandson, for lending himself and his canine companion Arnold to the story.

# Pollinating Terra

**Themes:** *Warrior* S. Salinas/R. Safinia; ***Flight of the Bumble Bee*** Rimsky-Korsakov

*"This is a new day, fresh, untouched. What will we do with it?"*

-Native American Church

## Symbiotic Parasites: Killers or Healers?

*The word parasite is from the Greek word meaning, "the one that eats at the table of others". It is s estimated to be from around 5900 BC.*

*Parasites are a varied group of organisms that are smaller than their host organism and reproduce faster by damaging and eventually killing the host. A lethal virus like Covid-19 only comes to life once inside the host, us. They receive benefits like food and shelter from the host, allowing them to multiply and spread throughout the body.*

*Still, in some cases, both species benefit from the interaction and this is known as mutualism. The larger organism is considered a host because, in a symbiotic relationship, it is the larger organism on which the smaller organism depends. The smaller organism is considered to be a symbiont that lives inside the host. Here the parasite gains benefits from the host which in turn harms the host without killing it. The number of parasites exceeds the number of free-living organisms, meaning that the parasitic lifestyle has been successful.*

*Sure, parasites destroying the host kill themselves as well. But is just not killing the host the best that can happen? How about healing?*

*"Gut flora, or the slew of microorganisms that live in your gut are bacteria that have a lot more influence over our behavior than we ever imagined. First discovered in mice gut bacteria modulate mood, cognition, even pain, but this has also been confirmed in humans. Without our gut bacteria humans are at a severe disadvantage, besides extracting a few essential nutrients they also help fight off infectious bacteria, even modulate the immune system directly."*

*Oct 28 '19 John 67k1212 gold badges9999 silver badges224*

As to our Earth: Who are Gaia's Parasites?

## Attraction in Reverse

I grew up in the early 1940s of the last century. From age four on, we were mostly outdoors on our own. Especially on non-school days in the summer and on weekends.

At age three, I told my mother I was running away from home due to some perceived injustice now forgotten. She was fine with this, just reminding me that I wasn't allowed to cross the street by myself yet. I accepted this regulation and gathered my voyage necessities. This was solely a red wagon carrying a loaf of bread and a jar of peanut butter. My launch was successful. While my mother watched from the front door and waved goodbye, I drove my red wagon to the outer limits of my freedom. There, at the curb, I had to stop. I was not allowed to cross the street by myself yet. Reflecting, I realized that in only another year or two I would be old enough to go anywhere by myself. Mission postponed until then. Much like what happened a lifetime later with GRD space travel.

In those earliest days of childhood freedom, we roamed as we chose, just returning for meals or sleep. Our toys matched this freedom.

One of mine was a dart gun. You just cocked it and the rubber sheath inside stretched so a dart could be shot out. Came with a target and safe darts with rubber suction tips. How long for us seven year olds to remove the rubber suction tips from the darts and just shoot the metal darts. Shoot them anywhere. How much longer to shoot other things like nails or thumb tacks, BBs (the 1940s equivalent of birdshot). The fields behind our home had grass taller than we were. So now I could stalk the overgrown jungle, with my lethal toy, able to defend myself against the wealthier children stalking with real BB guns, air rifles. Somehow only frogs were shot in these battles, a luckier time.

Maybe just as well. The frogs were from a creek that flowed from the highly polluted Lake Erie. The steel factory runoff had killed all fish and other life in the Lake, filling our stream with strychnine. And yet, some of the frogs survived. Some had reverted enough to have teeth.

Another toy was a friend's tire pump, "borrowed" from his father. This we used to pump air into large glass bottles in the fields until they exploded. No flying glass shards penetrated any of us. Another childhood miracle.

I had already explored the wonders of a household clothes presser. It had a huge roller to flatten pants or shirts. Since both of my parents worked, I had free reign to press anything in the roller that I would feed it. My hands survived though. Some close calls.

The last and most relevant toy from those years was not meant as a toy. It was a vacuum cleaner. The vacuum cleaner was the most interesting. What I really appreciated was that it had a reverse option. Flick a switch and it shot out the vacuumed contents wherever you wanted them to go.

So I did my vacuuming chore, sucking dirt into the vacuum bag. Also, down in the underground level cellar, spiders, ants, flies, and other small sized life forms. Not to mention food crumbs and anything else small enough to be captured.

Once the bag was full, I used an extension cord to move this amazing vacuum into our yard.

Next door was a family that had a well-tended vegetable garden. They were so protective of their greens that they routinely threw rocks at us children in the fields whenever we got close. Their son had an air rifle and he shot at us routinely.

Actually killed a little girl's kitten when it had only been curious about exploring their garden (kittens never eat their vegetables and look at how healthy they are)(unless shot). Biting frogs were one thing but her kitten was another.

So I put our vacuum in reverse and shot the bag's filthy crawling contents across the fence and into their garden. Often. A cold case serial crime never solved.

Vacuums with the reverse option are hard to find in this century. Still, the principle propelled Erik and his passengers to Mars.

## Discovery of the Gravity Repulsion Drive (GRD or "Gerd")

*"What is a magnet repulsion? Magnetic force, attraction or repulsion that arises between electrically charged particles because of their motion. It is the basic force responsible for such effects as the action of electric motors and the*

*attraction of magnets for iron." magnetic force | Definition, Formula, Examples, & Facts | Britannica www.britannica. com/science/magnetic-force*

And: "*Mass is not like charge, it cannot be either positive or negative, it is always positive and thus **Newtonian gravity** is always attractive. OK, in Newtonian gravity the gravitational force is always attractive because mass is always positive.*"

"*Why is gravitational force always attractive in nature?*" In the Physics Forums Insight Blog.

*Always* attractive? What about this: "

*In contrast to the **attractive force between two objects with opposite charges**, two objects that are of like charge will repel each other. That is, a positively charged object will exert a repulsive force upon a second positively charged object. This repulsive force will push the two objects apart.*" --Physics Tutorial: Charge Interactions www.physicsclassroom.com/class/estatics/Lesson-1/Charge-Interactions

And here was another classic mistake:

"*Does gravity ever repel? This simple answer is that gravity is only ever observed to be an attractive force. Unlike the electric force where charges can be both positive and negative and either attract or repel depending on the difference in charge, there is no such thing as negative mass. All massive objects attract each other.* ***Gravity never acts to repel two objects****.*" (Their bolding emphasis.)

*Does gravity push or pull? | Socratic* socratic.org/questions/does-gravity-push-or-pull

Wrong.

Because:

*"The only repulsive force that arises in similar cosmological discussions is one due to dark energy - or the cosmological constant, to be more specific. Dark energy is something very different than dark matter. This force makes the expansion of the Universe accelerate and it is due to the negative pressure of dark energy which may be argued to cause this "repulsive gravity". However, dark energy is not composed of any particles. It's just a number uniformly attached to every volume of space."* Apr 30 '11 at 17:18 Luboš Motl *170k1414 gold badges369369 silver badges581*

Dark energy is the force expanding our universe, an observed expansion now very clear to physicists. Powerful enough?

Let's move forward a few decades in the later 21st century when dark energy is better understood. When it ***exactly*** illustrated the magnetic repulsive power of gravity fields.

From this, an essential application, the Gravity Repulsion Drive, the GRD or "Gerd" was invented.

No more rocket fuel needed. Earth to Mars in a day, a short commute.

Which is why Erik was piloting a team of archaeologists to Mars.

## Erik

Erik was born on November 2nd, 1987.

At the age of 40, he had become "*America's hero*".

In January of 2032, at the age of 45, he was chosen to be the pilot for earth's most essential trip to Mars.

His cargo of experts was decades younger. Their classified equipment was even younger, mostly technological infants invented for this purpose.

Not counting the communications equipment broadcasting constantly to earth's surviving human population. A recent invention made it instantaneous despite the distance.

For those reading this back in the earlier 21st century, let's take a closer look at just who Erik was.

Erik grew up in San Francisco. His father, Ben, was a psychologist and professor who also taught Tai Ch'i Chuan, Qigong, Health & Wellness Workshops. His mother, Lori, was equally gifted. Erik was their only child.

His childhood was usually happy.

Even when his godfather gave him “dragon boots” that added dragon growls to every footstep. The adults, including those living below their apartment, were not impressed.

Still, the memory lasted through the years.

His family, when he was very young, usually went to shows at Lake Tahoe in the summer. One show, particularly, stood out. An acrobatic troupe asked for a young volunteer from the audience to join them in a demonstration. Erik's hand shot up.

His godfather had already seen an earlier show and knew it was safe. This he shared with Erik's parents before they could say "*absolutely not!*" They were unconvinced but it was too late. Erik was chosen. In little time he was being tossed high into the air and photographed there laughing in delight. His parents were white knuckled but too young yet for stroke risk.

Young Erik returned to land gracefully, receiving audience applause all the way back to the original seats.

Around this time Erik (far right) identified, along with his friends, even further with acrobatic TV and movie heroes.

His father enrolled Erik in martial arts classes at which he soon excelled.

Not coincidentally for his parents, early martial arts training included safer ways to fall, avoiding injury.

His mind was as advanced as his body. Going to one of the most rigorous high schools in San Francisco, he graduated with the full support of his family and friends.

To his other side from his parents are godparents. The godfather is not sleeping but his eyes shut reflexively as photographs are taken.

Or so he insisted.

Erik developed a great interest in other species. Some were favorites.

Like most youth, he was fascinated by dinosaurs.

Or their descendants:

He sought more contemporary dragons than dinosaurs. In this, curiosity always substituted for fear.

Sometimes it was affection. Particularly with wolves.

And their descendants:

Erik graduated at a California university with a major in Exercise Physiology.

Notable was his graduation there when he followed his receipt of the diploma with a memorable backflip.

Not for the first time either.

Years of practice made this seem effortless although it had been far from that on the way.

Erik was already known for both his acrobatics and an uplifting wit including a relentless sense of humor. Both skills were effective with allies or opponents, in strategy or tactics.

At this point, Erik explored his career options.

What was a hero with skills and an empathic conscience to do?

He decided to become a San Francisco EMT, lifesavers with wheels.

And so he was for years.

Nor did he, in looking at who he was and who he wanted to be, ever forget where he came from.

Understanding his past, he lived his present fully.

Until he decided it was time to build a new future. Approaching a 30th birthday can do that.

He decided to join the U.S. Air Force as a paramedic.

White knuckles returned to family. The fundamental mission of a military is to "*kill the enemy*". How is this congruent with Erik?

Family debate ensued. Extensive family debate. Erik had become a great listener and this he did.

He also, as always, made his own decisions.

To Erik, the fundamental purpose of the paramedic is to save lives, not take them. As aware as he could be of the challenges of this path, he began it.

Besides, parachuting from a plane to *save* those lives was part of his flow.

Basic training was done easily.

Nobody though would ever call the subsequent paramedic qualification process as easy. "*Rigorous*" didn't begin to describe it. The space between challenge and torture came closer. Easier to become a Navy Seal, an Army Ranger, or a top Marine.

Most of those going through this with Erik were a decade younger or more. Waiting until his 30s had some advantages, but his body's vulnerability wasn't one of them. Early on a hard landing broke bones.

His trainers made sure he could try again when he healed. Like most people he met in life, they wanted him to succeed. "*They like my motivation and that I have a brain*" Erik explained.

His sense of humor got him through the recovery as always.

He had a few more goes at qualification marathons. Most never made it through but Erik completed the course and met the requirements each time. Only again and again to have the requirements raised just past his marks *after* the qualifications were done.

Who was moving the goalposts? To keep him out? He never knew.

But there were enough senior officers impressed by him to keep him in the game.

By the time he took his final shot to qualify, it no longer mattered.

He had been chosen for something far more important.

The UFO Identity Task Force (ITF).

By 2023 the military and global governments had formerly acknowledged the existence of UFOs. These moved faster than human bodies or the machines they fly could survive. They clustered around nuclear facilities, military bases, chased military jets. Moved randomly and disappeared at unbelievable speeds.

What were they?

Sorting through various options based on data from around the world, the UFO ITF spent three years trying to answer this question. It was Erik who noticed first.

*"Ever see people cluster around a bad car accident? UFOs seem to cluster like that about accidents ABOUT to happen. Why?"*

And: *"Their movements remind me of hummingbirds or dragonflies. A time rate much faster than ours, they can hover or just shoot out of frame. I think they are a life form, not a plane or ship. Possibly an augmented life form or a cyborg vehicle.*"

Plus: "*They're not using rocket fuel or any fuel. I think they are manipulating gravity.*"

The international data they had gathered supported all of this. Setting aside the 'why' and the 'who', some fundamental questions had answers.

Erik was given full credit for giving the next invented gravity repulsion drive its impetus. Even to its use to protect the pilot from gravity crushing during acceleration.

It was also Erik that used data found as early as the Mars Rover days in the late 2020s, to identify the shores of the dry lakebeds and nearby mountains on Mars as the best place to identify where life on ancient Mars might have gone.

## SIDEBAR: The beginning of the Sixth and Final Mass Extinction on Earth

Climate change on our own planet had driven our own population underground and into mountains. As global warming grew, the melted glaciers brought flooding, the heat with record fires. It was a positive feedback acceleration and it was worse than any scientific projection. Billions of refugees sought safe shelter.

None of the political and international attempts to curb the effect were remotely in time. Greed by the corporate polluters reversed all such attempts. Even then, most of the human family remained or were kept unaware of the extinction direction we were heading. They were told it would pass, it was a hoax, prayer would turn this around.

Soon the ambient heat of the day made inhabitation or commerce impossible. For a time human life, shopping, schools, entertainment, hospitals- All moved fully into the night where it was cooler. Daytime was abandoned to the intense heat.

When, in only a decade, that no longer worked, underground survivor settlements were needed. Military installations like NORAD built into and under the Rockies had long been around but now they hugely expanded. Corporate executives seemed to prefer the Swiss Alps.

Ominously the layer of breathable atmosphere was thinning.

## Back to Erik

Well, you know, or will know in time, the rest of his story.

What matters here is that his leadership in developing the gravity repulsion drive and in identifying the best places on Mars to find ancient life came together to generate global demand.

Erik was the obvious choice to pilot the ship bringing the young archaeologists and their brand new devices to Mars.

And so it was.

Corporate magnates benefitting from centuries of planetary pollution, even then opposed Erik's ventures, especially the Mars trip.

Most influential of these was a trillionaire we will call Magnum Bolus.

The Bolus family, safely ensconced in the Swiss Alps, for the time being, did all they could to stop Erik's trip from going forward.

Magnum's wife, Karen Bolus, used her former acting experience to generate fears about what Erik was *really* about. But by then, most surviving humans knew better. Erik was humanity's best hope.

## The Trip

Pushing off from earth always gave a great view.

Erik magnified this to better show something important to the crew and the world population following them on

TV monitors back home. Such a thin layer of atmosphere and getting thinner. All on land so slim compared to the earth's bulk that it has been compared to an eggshell. (See the Nelson Bond story "*Lo the Bird*")

Amplifying the gravity repulsion from earth, the ship shot suddenly far into space, racing toward their goal. While humanity watched. Only a trailing UFO managed to keep pace.

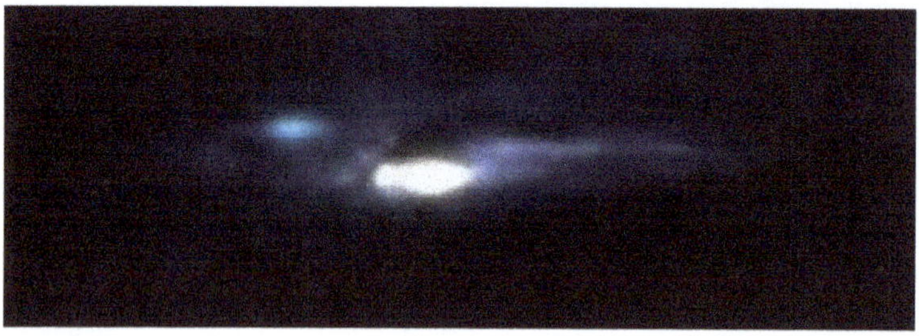

The destination came into sight.

A circuit around the planet allowed the archeological instruments to locate the best landing site for their work: a dry lake bed surrounded by huge mountains.

Mars seemed as though it had burned to a cinder. Another mass extinction?

## Terraforming Mars from Afar

Back at the in-mountain NORAD complex back on earth, Erik had been part of a key group charged with making Mars more possible to earth human immigrants, terraforming it.

This was done from far away earth at first. Plants and trees compatible with the Mars atmosphere were sent there by unmanned vehicles, crashing into a region found to have huge reservoirs of underground water. Most of this greenery with cell walls, earth trees and plants, survived. Converting substantial amounts of air to their byproducts of breathable oxygen.

Human colonies, adequately sheltered, so colonized the region. They adapted quickly. Before long the catch became clear. The low gravity of Mars did not prepare them for the higher gravity of earth. The hearts of Mars inhabitants rarely survived any home visits to their larger and hotter mother planet. They were confined to the Mars colony for life.

Back at the NORAD complex, it was clear that an actual earth-like planet must be found, colonized. A new start. And this was done sooner than expected. From there, the challenge was getting to it.

## A Millennium Hero *(Transcript from the beamed broadcast)*

Narrator (N): "*No argument exists any longer. This 21st century pioneer stands out as our millennium hero, finding that survival path to Mars and beyond. The new home for our human family: Terra.*"

*"Erik Tong's own history is well known. Born in San Francisco as the only child of universally respected and loved professor of psychology Benjamin Tong, with his equally impressive mother Lori Tong. He grew up with an added two Godfathers and, now, as many claiming to be his cousins as grains of sand on Ocean Beach. He trained in martial arts and excelled at a top high school. We have followed his university degree in exercise physiology to long service as an EMT, through a path toward a paramedic career in the US Air Force, and then a diversion from that path to the US Navy. On the way he acquired real estate in Texas, California, and New Mexico sufficient to develop his financial empire. By the time he had finished with his military career, he had enough capital to found his New Mexico research center, nearby what eventually became the International Space Port that Star Trek had always predicted would be there. From that time, he led space travel into its new era, developing an entirely unique alternative space travel methodology, twice, and after that Captained the flight that has brought us via Mars and beyond to great hope for us all today."*

(Music bridge ends, broadcast interview begins.)

N: *Erik Tong has kindly consented to this interview with the request that we refer to his responses in any beamed communication as coming from "ET", an endearing form of address his father liked to use for him. This transmission is being beamed to Earth from Terra via a quantum connection at Mars just one year after our arrival there Here we go.*

N: *How did you invent the first gravity drive?*

ET: *No welcome Erik? (Laugh) Okay. It began when I liked geometry class better than the algebra class. I read that Albert Einstein got ideas in his mind in pictures, not math. Then his wife, not known enough in history, translated many of them into math equations so other physicists could understand. I'm no Einstein but I do often get my own ideas, and solve problems, in mental pictures. There is a balance in nature. Whatever exists has an opposite. Big planets have lots of gravity pull, small ones less, space none.*

N: *Unless the space station or ship is rotated.*

ET: *That's right. Rotation can supply gravity. Which tells you its more complicated than we thought. The opportunity is that the rotation creates local gravity which could protect the people inside from acceleration and G-forces that would otherwise be crushing, another application. But back to the point. I saw in my mind that there must be a negative gravity, a push rather than a pull. There if we look for it.*

N: *And you found it.*

N: *Me and my team. Found it, found a way to go back and forward, positive and negative gravity waves. Engineered a drive to make use of it on a ship.*

N: *No more explosive propulsion rockets.*

ET: *Blowing up things, shooting things, lots of fun for a lot of people. OUR ships were too silent, unimpressive.*

N: *Less expensive?*

ET: *That too. Helped but annoyed a lot of vested interests. The old way made some very rich people richer. We pushed through but not easily.*

N: *For quite a while your new access to the asteroids and then to Mars made some new people rich. You too I think.*

ET: *Definitely. We accumulated enough to bypass the financial gravity of greedy billionaires holding us back.*

N: *You eventually found a second even better use for your gravity drive.*

ET: *Once physicists realized that the universe was full of dark matter, meaning not visible, it became a prime mystery. On top of that was dark energy, a force pushing galaxies farther apart over time, accelerating to expand distances rather than a force winding down or imploding. Another mystery.*

N: *You visualized this?*

ET: *Well, my main interest was improving our gravity drive. But what I saw was that all the mass from dark matter was generating its own reverse gravity, a push rather than a pull.*

N: *Which in your ship you could use with your forward or reverse gravity drive.*

ET: *You've been paying attention!*

N: *I try. True though, much of this is already known about that breakthrough.*

ET: *Not known or experienced was how long it took, the engineering involved, the tons of money needed. Dark energy as reverse gravity, the ultimate drive. In the end, we got it to work. Now we had an intergalactic drive. We could go anywhere.*

N: *If you lived long enough.*

ET: *Well, that puzzle was solved by the UFOs.*

N: *After all those sightings on Earth, you made first contact with them on Mars!*

ET: *Well, once there, we did stand out. With Earth on a path to become as burned up as Mars, they naturally assumed we were ready for a new home.*

N: *They?*

ET: *Not our planet-bound living UFOs. These were from another place and time. Still, they admired our initiative, cheered us on in what they assumed was our ultimate destination. A fresh start on a new Earth-like planet. Once we fully understood this, we realized that they were right.*

N: *More on who 'they' were?*

ET: *Another story. There and then they shared the map, allowing us to travel impossible distances by worm-hole short cuts. It was like a map I saw once in Palau on how ancient Pacific Islanders navigated the ocean's hazards. This map though, using our drive, allowed interstellar travel. Especially now to Terra, the Earthlike planet we are here to colonize.*

N: *Colonize? Or infest?*

ET: *Pollinate! We have found no life forms here so far that are a threat to us. We're being very careful. Think of our arrival as like a colony of bees, here to pollinate the flowers.*

N: *What about your impact on the whole planet itself?*

ET: *We take the fate of Mars and soon Earth to heart. This is another chance and we are taking it. This time not as parasites but as symbionts. In a home we must protect.*

N: *Any words for those on Earth still able to receive this?*

ET: *If you can join us here, come ahead and be welcome. But come with respect for the planet of our second chance, our unspoiled Terra, ready to be pollinated and thrive.*

N: *So we WON'T ruin this planet all over again! No more mass extinction. WE control who comes here. Symbionts welcome! Parasites not! Our human family has learned its lesson by now. This time, sure and certain survival. Guaranteed! Right?*

ET: *Well...*

End of transmission.

# ELIZA EARP

**Themes:** *Netherlands Harmonica/Once upon a Time in the West* Ennio Morricone; *Gunfighter* Eric Kissack/ narrated by Nick Offerman

## Doc Holliday

Little Dolly Day Holliday loved her name. In the early grades she refused to shorten it into a nickname, reciting every syllable.

Once a teacher threatened to drop her off alone miles into the high desert if she didn't stop doing that.

The class spontaneously voted unanimously in favor of the trip but to no avail.

Dolly Day Holliday also loved her father's claim that she was distantly related to the infamous Doc Holliday.

She idolized him young  and as an older legend.

That dentist, gunfighter, gambler, outlaw, and deputy to Wyatt Earp died at age 36 from the tuberculosis he caught from his mother while caring for her.

Doc spread so many fantastic stories about himself, that he became a western hero, even to this day.

Even to very young Dolly Day Holliday who determined to add "Doc" to her name.

Fanning this initially cute fantasy, her father got her a child-size 1-caliber gun with rubber-tipped bullets.

Which she always wore when she could.

Though the little bullets just annoyed people when they hit.

## ELIZA

**ELIZA** was an early natural language processing computer program created from 1964 to 1966 at the MIT Artificial Intelligence Laboratory by Joseph Weizenbaum. It was meant to prove that intelligent communication from machines to humans was not happening, just a superficial mistake.

In 1997 IBM pitted their best computer, named *Deep Blue*, against a world class chess master. *Deep Blue* won. Decades later, *Blue* still enjoys that distant glory. Though he never found a way for it to compensate him personally.

In modern times, Google invented a deep learning model, *AlphaGo*, to beat top Go board game players.

ELIZA simulated conversation by using a "pattern matching" and substitution methodology that gave users an illusion of understanding on the part of the program. A precursor to today's *Siri*, *Alexa*, and others, it had no built in framework for contextualizing events. Directives on how to interact were provided by "scripts", written to have ELIZA seem to process user input by conscious reflective response, but actually ELIZA was just following the rules and directions of the script.

The most famous script, DOCTOR, sounded like a Rogerian psychotherapist (Carl Rogers, who was well satirized for repeating to patients what they had just said, but actually with skill for leading them to greater healing depth).

ELIZA was to use script rules to respond with non-directional questions to user inputs. As such, ELIZA was one of the first chatterbots and one of the first programs capable of attempting the Turing test of mechanical awareness. ELIZA's creator, Weizenbaum, thought his program would discourage belief in intelligent communication from machine to human. Instead he was shocked by the number of individuals who attributed human-like feelings to his computer program, including his own secretary.

Many academics believed that the program would be able to help many people, particularly with psychological issues, and that it could be an aid to doctors.

While ELIZA was actually capable of engaging in scripted discourse, users were often convinced of ELIZA's intelligence and understanding, despite Weizenbaum's urging that this was not genuine insight. Still, ELIZA became famous as a catalyst for discussion on consciousness or the self- awareness of the most sophisticated machines. Some urged these machines be represented by lawyers in court to assert their rights. (The toasters had no comment.)

Dolly Day Holliday had studied the Shinto religion when visiting Japan. From that she acknowledged the life force in all things, rocks included, though conscious reflective awareness varied. So acknowledging awareness in the most complex advanced sophisticated robots was no stretch for her.

Tired of proving the obvious, she had an insight. It would seem though, that the ELIZA test was focused backwards, entirely on the wrong group.

## ELIZA EARP

After her college graduation, Dolly Day Holliday pursued and completed her MD, with a dual major in Psychology with an emphasis on Advanced Neuroscience Computer Technology.

Skipping over the 'Dentist' aspect of her legendary idol, she 'upgraded' the legend to resurrect it by now naming her PhD self as legitimately "Doc Holliday".

That name stuck. Or else.

Now her insight about ELIZA turned into a driven purpose. In this, Doc Holliday was persuasive, despite her quirky cowboy boots and the perpetual holstered firearm (now 45 caliber).

That plus her Texas location did in fact gain her substantial grants to rebuild and redirect a newer ELIZA. More robot than machine. It took two very well-funded years. She also insistently upgraded the name of her creation to ELIZA EARP. The EARP stood for *Evident Awareness Realistically Proven.* Still annoying the sceptics.

The press, of course, still called her robot just plain ELIZA. Skipped the EARP for quite a while.

They even added fanciful illustrations of ELIZA EARP including one of child Doc Holliday with a machine ELIZA EARP at a high school Science Fair.

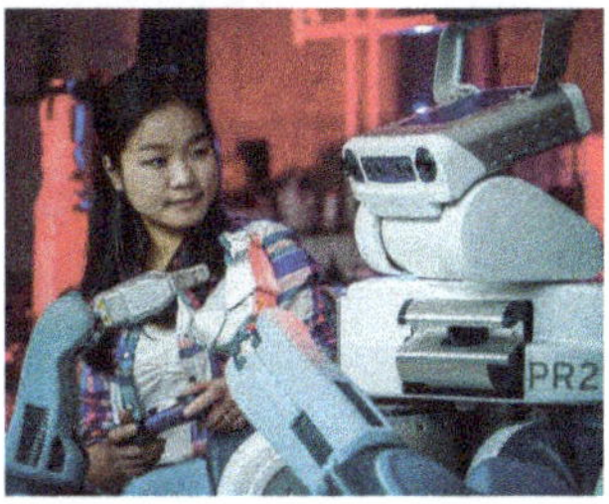

Doc Holliday loved their other image and made it so.

After field testing on ever more intelligent robotic machines, with consistently convincing evidence of their consciousness, she finally redirected public discussion to focus on an overlooked group of interactors: Humans.

Some humans were clearly conscious and self-aware. Possibly more than a few were not. Just attend to the daily news.

So: what was the range of intelligent awareness of people? How many could not pass the computer test and prove that they were conscious individuals? And, more controversial, who could not?

Here Doc Holliday, as the media now happily agreed to call her, showed great diplomatic tact.

She told the press she wished to first give her creation a "*data ceiling*" using input from a most distinguished group, the "*clear leaders of American humanity*". The United States Congress.

Flattery prevailed and the two majority leaders of House and Senate committed to participation for each and every member of Congress.

A flattered Republican National Committee (RNC) mandated additional participation from the justices of the Supreme Court (SCOTUS).

The executive branch (POTUS) insisted on participating as well, core staff included.

On the day of distinguished input, the actual data collection was swift.

Assuming that the attention span of participants might be very low, especially once the press and TV photo ops were done, Doc Holliday had been able to promise that the actual data collection could be done in 30 seconds (the exact length of the gunfight in the OK Corral). Her robot had developed direct inter-communication with the participant cortex such that a barrage of questions with returning answers was almost simultaneous.

Doc Holliday had also simultaneous input collectors for each and every distinguished government participant, all gathered in the huge cavernous Arizona Conference Room reserved for the event.

The individual sets of earphones and microphones poured in the multitude of responses to ELIZA EARP in her undisclosed location.

No problem for the famous genius robot as the tidal wave of data was digested. The analysis began very soon after.

The results were quickly funneled to the robot from Doc Holliday's gun-shaped remote in her holster. (The 45 caliber gun long since replaced.)

By the time everybody was done, just 30 seconds for even the slowest political dignitaries, she was out and past the outside press through a secret underground exit.

Moving quickly, before the global and domestic press lost interest, she released a complete report to them through the internet, copies open sourced to the world.

The results overall showed quite a range. There was indeed a ceiling for some of the brightest respondents. There was also a substantial baseline for so many low-scoring people, clearly more unaware than a toaster.

One party had more of these *"toaster level"* politicians than the other. (Toasters popped up in independent protest to this demeaning term all over the world. As ever, their protest pops went unheeded.)

This toaster level result for so many highly visible leaders was shocking to some but no surprise for most of the world. Even the POTUS staff and SCOTUS justices had found some toaster level individuals in their ranks. Again, little surprise as to who these were, but much shock at being outed by ELIZA EARP.

The press wanted to interview Doc Holliday all about this event, now termed by them as "*The OK Corral*" testing in that Arizona Conference Room. Since the testing had taken the same 30 seconds the original gunfight had, the similarity held very well. Even to the original gunfight being in the Arizona town of Tombstone, while ELIZA EARP had this time unearthed legions of political tombstones.

Doc Holliday had become the most famous person to not be seen again through all the furor.

So many people outed as being dumb as toasters had resigned or otherwise exited. The country then began to soar with the more aware and competent leadership. Entering into a happier golden era. Next, the open source distribution to all the countries in the world produced parallel results: international leaders outed as toaster level lost power.

Doc Holliday was not there to be thanked. She would have just credited ELIZA EARP for all the sweet outcomes. It was true. ELIZA EARP had found Doc a new secret laboratory where new discoveries could be made. At least whenever Doc could get ELIZA EARP to stop laughing.

Turned out this very aware robotic machine loved irritating the people that deserved it, even more than Doc Holliday did.

**Note:** This was the third of four stories excerpted from *Time Statue Dreams* with permission.

# Aye or Nay

**Theme:** *Bad Moon Rising* Credence Clearwater Revival

Well, a UFO finally landed, this time in New Mexico, and made contact.

The US Space Force was first to surround the ship with TV media not far behind.

The Space Force sent their chiefs to an invited diplomatic dinner, one catered by the spaceship's aliens. This was to be televised live for the world.

Conspiracy theorists had some interesting fears about what would happen.

The Space Force brass on site was not deterred. They seemed happy for the TV audience.

In the kitchen, the space aliens were prepared. The chef was backed up by an interpreter of earth culture and its languages. Also there was a high tech expert who could materialize any food dish on earth that would be requested.

The chef herself approached the table, nodded to the TV cameras, smiled at their primitive technology, and requested orders.

The Space Force leader said: "*Do you have any suggestions?*" Very diplomatic.

With her language interpreter in her mind, the chef said "*Of course. We will choose a meal for you, one suiting an occasion like this, a dinner special you might say.*"

The space force admiral in charge considered this.

Finally asking the group around the table to each say if that was their choice, affirmative or negative.

He nodded to the lowest ranking officer to begin, anticipating that he, as the leader would go last.

One at a time the officers declined saying "*Nay*".

As this answer worked its way around the table, it at finally came to the top ranked admiral to respond.

He was glad he had waited until the last. He understood that the rest were ethnocentric and were afraid of being expected to eat alien-chosen food sight unseen.

But he at least knew this was a diplomatic mission. And it was on live TV.

So he said, loud and clear: "*Aye*". Smiling proudly at his unique courage and leadership, all on display to the viewing world.

Back in the kitchen, the chef was puzzled at what to do. She and her interpreter had expected a "*yes*" or a "*no*".

Her tech expert knew not what earth dishes to materialize.

The interpreter though intervened with her usual unwarranted confidence.

She explained that in American cultural language, "*Nay*" was the sound a horse makes.

So all those saying that word expected a well prepared dish that would please a horse.

The other one "*Aye*" order referred to the organ for sight.

Now the tech alien was happy.

She knew the dishes associated with each of these requests.

She would materialize them with diplomatic dining style.

And soon all at the table were served.

For those requesting "*Nay*", a large center piece of fresh grass was placed on the table:

Each of the "*Nay*" officers was then served an individual entree of grazing grass in a bowl and a feedbag filled with oats.

And a second larger feedbag for the table to make sure they had enough oats:

As a side dish, raw carrots were supplied.

Finally, the chef had creatively combined the beverage with dessert, producing a green grass smoothie for each guest.

Added was the horse laxative to aid digestion.

This left the highest ranking admiral, truly by now a legend in his own mind.

Of course he already had the same beverage everybody else had, delicious.

But what grand entrée would his "*Aye*" order bring? The TV cameras focused on him as his order arrived.

The alien tech in collaboration with the chef had materialized two dishes from France and another from Indonesia.

All with key bovine optical ingredients. Eyes of a cow.

The television ratings were the highest ever measured.

- **Note:** This was the fourth and last of four stories excerpted from *Time Statue Dreams* with permission.

# Circe's Bacon

**Themes:** *Zorba the Greek* instrumental; *What's Going On?* Marvin Gaye

*"Circe made the men sit at her table and served them a mixture of cheese, barley and honey mixed in Pramnian wine. The men greedily drank, unaware that she had mixed some of her special drugs into the mixture. Once they had finished drinking, Circe struck them with her wand, turning them into pigs and driving them into pigsties."*
*-The Odyssey*

At first it was a tiny speck at the top of our mountain. As daylight shifted it was somewhere between copper and bronze with a green outline. As I watched, it seemed to be growing, meaning it was coming closer.

Meaning it was up to me to see what it was. To see if it was a threat or at least a problem.

I spoke into the air, asking Homer, our supercomputer, to put the speck on a monitor screen, enlarged. He complied.

It had stopped moving. It was a statue apparently, of a naked bronzed young woman wearing only a loose green shawl. Her arms were raised to the heavens.

What had caused that movement before?

No! Not a statue. Her arms moved down and she looked right in my direction. Began walking toward my building.

Homer said she was a live person but not a threat. Said, strangely, that she belonged here, that she was safe to let in.

I thanked Homer and told him to go back to sleep.

Unlocked the front door electronically. Opened it.

Waited.

## Odie

Me? I work here. Security and science in that order. This is a secret facility. It doesn't officially exist.

We all have self-selected names that our parents wouldn't recognize. In this place they call me Odie (said as "Oh-Dee").

Well, kind of self-selected. We selected to let Homer decide. DNA analysis and all, he knows us fully. Also has an intriguing sense of humor. Not often understood right away. I think of it as time-release irony.

So yes, he named me Odysseus Veni. Still considering why. Meantime I'm just Odie.

We're on a remote Pacific Island. A small mountain divides it. Gives us elevation where our complex rests near the top.

If I do the short walk to the highest point, the view is magnificent facing the other side. Ocean in the distance and a few miles of undeveloped greenery between. Except for that pig farm.

This scenic beauty makes my eyes happy. My nose not so much. An overcrowded pig farm mass produces a sweet-smelling shit odor so strong it even hits me when here.

The pig farm has been here longer than we have. Provided protein to the island region surrounding us for generations. We bought from it as well once we were established here.

When the last pig farm owner died, one of our project founders, Homer- named Magnum Bolus, bought it and retired there. Possibly being devoid of a sense of smell.

Most of the year our complex is full of scientists. Converting our supercomputer, Homer, into quantum mode. Working often around the clock, inspired by the creative but exhausting work.

But this is the month of August. Led by the Europeans on staff, they all vacation the entire month. Leaving only Homer and me to secure the facility.

Homer is great company when I want it. Including martial arts lessons. I had thought I was an adept at that. But he's showing me amazing things that I didn't know my body could do. Ki magnified.

Homer has had a few dark outs but always provided explanations on return.

Once he let me know of a series of small energy drains that turned out to be just a back door link to founder Magnus. Seems, retired or not, he still was using our computer resources. For what? Maybe more than the wellbeing of pigs. I'll look more into this when the staff gets back.

The other times Homer explained that he was following a directive to develop his quantum capacity. This includes letting in the quantum entangled components to enlarge his reach. Entanglement by definition means a connection at any distance. Maybe from other planets, stars, galaxies? Hope Homer remains Homer.

Homer says entanglement occurs as a connection through a higher dimension, one independent of our world's distance. Some as old as th beginning of our universe.

More for the staff to review on their arrival.

Then he gives me a weather report. Tells a joke he knew I'd laugh at.

Okay still Homer. I think.

Well, my guest has entered.

**Circe**

She was shaking, glowing a reddish shade, seemed upset. Took off her only clothes, that green shawl, threw some surgical gloves from its pocket at me, and rushed to the little room off the entrance. The one I used for sleeping when on a long project night. Seemed to know her way. Not saying a word.

I followed.

She was already face down on the bed. On her knees. More shaking, like a vibrating.

She said "*Hurry!*"

The urgency in her voice included a sultry tone that almost mesmerized me.

Who was this overwhelmingly beautiful naked woman on my bed? What emergency was I supposed to rescue her from?

She gestured to her vagina and simply said in a plaintive voice "*Pull it out! I can't stand it anymore!*"

Something hurting her there. Talk later. I pulled on the gloves, lubricated them, and reached into her.

The obstacle felt like a fat thermometer, throbbing a little. It came out.

I put it in a shielded container. The kind we keep for possible explosives or other hazards. Returned to her.

She was still in the same position, the shaking subdued but still there. Her red glow remained, mainly stronger.

I put my hand on her back to comfort her but her shivering grew worse.

I asked "*What can I do to help you now?*"

She reached around with one hand and caressed me through my scrubs.

By then I was shivering too.

I did as she clearly wanted. Me too.

A time without measure went by.

We woke under the covers. I was holding her. Neither of us were shaking any more. The glow was more golden now. Both of us.

I didn't need to ask.

She said in her own calm unique voice "*I can explain now.*"

And a deeper "*Thank you.*"

## Circe's Tale

She began: "*The classic Circe loved Odysseus. She granted his wish to have his crew returned from pig form to human. To do this she went to the pig sty but could not discern which ones were his crew. Odysseus advised her to return them all to human form and his crew would come to him. This was done. As expected, his crew, somewhat confused, ran to be with their captain. But when Circe turned to deal with the other men, they were no longer in sight. She*

*just used her power, now nearly exhausted, to scatter them away from her island to all around the world. Some of these were pleased to be back in human form. Most though had been pigs, never human, and were stunned to be in human form now."*

Circe paused, hugged me, and continued.

*This is a departure from the actual Odyssey, as you can tell, but it does provide an explanation of my own as to why so many men act like pigs in human form. Magnum was one such swine, drawn to his own at the Pig Farm.*

She shuddered but took a breath and went on.

*Not you, Odysseus Veni.*

I looked like I was going to ask her how she knew my name but she put a finger on my lips and I was quiet. She continued.

*And finally I understand why Homer gave me this name and now you. He seems to love Greek classic myths. Lucky for me.*

*Kind of late, but anyway I should introduce myself. I was born with the given name of Circe Borgia. Raised at first in Peru where my mother's family had been for generations. Hence the skin color. My mother's family was originally Italian. But with the deserved notoriety of her ancestor, Lucretia Borgia, a branch of the family moved to another continent where nobody knew them. Or cared. I think Homer or his own powerful ancestors took an interest in us long before I was born. Yes, my name came from him my mother told me. And her own. In Homeric irony, I think it was irony, at her birth she was named Listeria Borgia. She claimed Homer was my father though I always thought she just didn't want to name the actual human rascal.*

A sigh. An unexpected kiss. Dazed, I gladly nodded my support for her to keep on.

*Listeria relocated us to Hawaii when I was 12. Went to the university there and studied everything but eventually took my doctoral degree in animal communication. Did you know that Dolphins not only speak but can also broadcast direct experience? Broadcast waves are not words. Ask your TV.*

She was happy now. Recalling a time in her life when it was always fun.

*So I took a job at a San Diego zoo. Famous place. My assignment as 'Dr. Borgia' was with the primates. Especially with one of the largest gorillas ever seen. Not King Kong size but easily seven feet tall if he could stand up. But at that weight he could not stand up. Zoo named him 'Kong' but not bestowing any royal title like 'King' to go with it.*

She laughed, continued.

*Kong easily learned to sign when I taught him. One of his first signs was 'happy', another was 'fun' and of course his special treat of 'grapes'. First sentence was 'Want happy, fun, grapes.' Accompanied at times by gorilla versions of laughing, growling, belching, and grooming.*

She smiled at this happy memory. I waited for her to catch her breath. I began brushing her hair with my hands, pretending to eat something I found there. She laughed but went on. Big momentum forward.

*As days went by he got much better at the vocabulary of signing and we had regular conversations. Sat together on the highest rock plateau where we could see over the encircling wall to the crowd.*

*We were interrupted often by zoo patrons who loved watching him, us.*

*Sometimes the worst were throwing things at us or making caustic remarks, especially when he carefull groomed me or brushed my hair.*

*Some seemed to think it was an inter-species affair, an offense to their hopeless values. Kong understood, was irritated by this, signed he was worried my feelings were being hurt by this disrespect.*

*I assured him I was fine, urged him just make it 'fun' and be 'happy'.*

*Kong considered this. Then asked me to bring him 'grapes', no, 'BIG grapes'.*

Here Circe looke at me with a big smile and a look that said something special was coming.

*I brought him, as fast as I could, a bunch of the largest I could find. He plucked two of these, now one in each hand, and placed one in each of his enormous nostrils.*

*The rude guys watching had their phones out for video recording. Laughing. Kong removed the grapes, moist with his mucous, one in each hand, and skillfully threw them at fastball speed.*

*At two of the worst patrons. Hit perfectly in their face. Splattered.*

*Now the crowd was silent. Kong took a bunch of the grapes, turned his rear to moon the crowd, and put them up his behind. Gasps from the crowd.*

*Then he pulled them out and aimed the grapes at the crowd. They ran.*

*Kong scored some impressive on-target long range shots anyway.*

*Laughed his Gorilla chortle, signed 'Fun' and then 'Happy!'.*

Quiet for a moment. Then-

*Well, the videos went viral and the zoo had lawsuits. I was fired with regrets.*

*Thanks to Homer, I still am in touch with Kong just not actually touching any more.*

*Homer? Oh, all my life he was a whisper in my ear. At crtical times like this especially. He does act like a father when I need one.*

*And at that time he told me I should take a new job as a lab assistant with a scientist named 'Magnum'.*

*Magnum was doing animal communication with pigs. Next to the world's most powerful SuperComputer. Exciting.*

*Which brought me to this island a year ago."*

She turned into my arms then and napped. I knew it would be best if I just waited this out. She had been through a lot and I was far from fresh. Eventually we both woke up, she hugged me and, without any pause, resumed exactly where she had ended.

*Turned out he wasn't interested in learning what the animals had to say. He just wanted them to obey his own communications.*

*My new job smelled awful. All the time. Magnum cared not at all for the pigs and left them crowded in terrible conditions.*

*All except for his research target, a huge male swine of at least a thousand pounds named 'Spurticus'. As he was the spurting constant progenitor of piglets, constantly humping the females or, disgustingly, urinating into the air above them, where the water-deprived sows would drink it.*

*Spurticus was a bully and in charge. Male piglets he killed. Their meat was sold by Magnum locally. Spurticus tolerated no rivals.*

*This was not a happy place to work but I did my best. Improved the conditions somewhat.*

*Magnum though, like Spurticus, was not open to any real change. Except for his research. There he listened."*

## Bacon

*"Homer told me to buy two large packages of bacon. On the island, this was from the male pigs slaughtered for their meat.*

*The closest large grocery packed up the meat and then I brought the packages back to the lab.*

*Magnum was intrigued. Said I must have had a reason for this impulse. I shrugged. Put one package in a freezer. He took the other one.*

*He had an idea. Starved Spurticus for a day and then tossed him some bacon.*

*The meat Spurticus caught was clearly from his own porcine family and he knew it. But he wolfed it down just the same. Then dozed.*

*Still, Magnum waited and watched. I took a shift.*

*On waking the huge pig was hungry again but Magnum held back any food, forbade me to feed him either. Now this was his research."*

Circe looked uncomfortable now. She was clearly getting to more recent trauma.

*Okay. This part is hard for me. But. I had helped Magnum invent a unique recording device. It looked like an oversize thermometer with pores.*

*It measured far more than temperature. Dispatched to us all the health measures we would ever want, some key mood indicators, and some aspects of basic communications.*

*He kept one of the two we made for himself. Leaving it by his own specimen jar. In a lab corner sat a jar of his own skin, sperm, and blood samples that he had been analyzing with the SuperComputer. Hoping to extend his life indefinitely.*

*The other invention was for the huge Spurticus pig. It was capable, given the right imput, of magnifying its hormonal activity. It could make the pig sleepy, hungry, horny, or angry.*

*So it had been sewn into the pig for an onging permanent read-out. No consent had been taken."*

Circe took a series of deep breaths, squeezed my hand.

*Magnum now made the pig more hungry than he already was, and he added the hormone for angry. Threw the pig a single bacon strip over the protective fence. The pig ate it.*

*Enough bacon clues. The pig tore into the nearest sow and ate her.*

*I screamed and cried. Magnum tried to show me the read-outs of the dining swine's controlled emotions, communications. I wasn't interested."*

Pause with tears. Then determination to say it all.

*"I told him I quit!*

*Never had quit anything before. But a year was enough and now this?*

*Except to give me orders and tasks, he had mostly ignored me for all my time there. I was just the help.*

*He was often busy doing some mysterious talk with two of our long distance donors. Or he was secretly tapping into the SuperComputer.*

*Making my job as lonely as it was smelly.*

*But the sows and piglets loved me as I brought them food, water, space, and attention.*

*Now this!*

*I turned to go to my room and pack.*

*A strange smelling cloth covered my face. Chloroform? Stronger.*

*I passed out.*

*I woke face down on a lab table. My midsection was propped up on some pillows. My clothes were gone. Only my pocketed shawl on a chair in the corner. I could see the full glass bottle of whatever he had used to knock me out.*

*He was behind me. I tried to turn but my muscles were still gone.*

*Then I felt him slip something into my vagina. Oh. Felt like one of our thermometers. His!*

*Taking readings! What else?*

*I couldn't speak though I tried. Just a weak moan came out.*

*He noted the moan, saying "Not happy with the placement? I lubricated it first. No need to sterilize it. Just has been in my anus. Good readings though. Well, I could also slip it into your other opening."*

*I moaned again. Made it sound angry at least.*

*"Oh. No objections for where it already is? Doesn't matter. When we are done with this, I'll just feed you to Spurticus."*

*I moaned again. Angry and louder.*

*"Oh, once the sex hormones get you to the right level, you're going to beg me to take it out, replace it with my own large erection. Hadn't noticed you enough until now. Time for me."*

*He was not in my sight but I could hear him breathing heavily. Was he really going to rape me?*

*Then I felt a gush of hormones inside the vaginal walls. He was forcing me to better receive him once he took out the thermometer and substituted himself.*

*What then? Feed me to Spurticus? As he had said.*

*The hormones were working. I was shivering as sexual energy filled me.*

*Energy is energy. NOW I had my muscle control back.*

*I swung my leg wide, just enough, and knocked the glass bottle of knockout liquid to the floor. Glass shattered, liquid pooled and vapors rose.*

*He rushed to cover it but it got him first. Feel to the floor. Out.*

*I had to get away before the vapor got to me. I moved to the door and flung it open, wide. Slid into my shawl, grabbed some surgical gloves, and ran out the entrance. Grabbed his personal specimen jar as I flew by.*

*I didn't know how long he would be out. I had shut the door behind me to be sure the vapors would last longer for him.*

*I was so angry. I had to stop him while I could.*

*Undressed as I was, I went to the pig pen where Spurticus lived.*

*He was still there starving, except for the ravaged remains of his last eaten sow and assorted piglets.*

*I emptied the jar of Magnum's specimens where he could get to it. Added half the pack of raw bacon.*

*Spurticus rushed to it. For his special meal.*

*I left the entry door to his pen open, using what was left of the bacon pack to make a trail to the room where Magnum still lay.*

*The air in the room seemed clear now. I had no idea how long I had to get out.*

*I heard the heavy steps of that massive male pig coming behind me.*

*No time left. I ran outside to the trail leading over the mountain.*

*I heard behind me the grunts and eating noises of Spurticus tearing into his Magnum meal. Maybe a scream?*

*I was out on the trail. Up to the top of our mountain.*

*Stopped to raise my arms to, hopefully, reach Homer for advice. I was coming to his home if he would let me.*

*A whisper in my ear: "Yes." And your name.*

*I was still shaking with that continuing hormonal burst of sexual urgency. That thermometer had to come out!*

*But once again I used the sexual energy to get me to you.*

*The rest you know.*

## After

The local news brought us up to date. The remains of Magnus had been found in the pig pen along with the multitude of pig bones. It was assumed that Spurticus had killed Circe too, though no clear remains had been found. That huge pig was put to death immediately. Case closed.

So we were married. Both of us now working with Homer and staff. Shielded by the top secret nature of the project.

We made a great team the three of us, including Homer.

He asked us privately if we had any lasting questions before we moved ahead. This is how it went.

Circe: *What was Magnum doing with those two donors?*

Homer: *That's our next project. They are each the richest human in their side of the earth. They are increasingly controlling communications, law, and force. Accelerating the demise of the planet. The human family with it. Including them. One hope is that realizing that last part, we can actually work with them in common cause. Or not. But likely they will soon see that the planet will cremate them with eveerybody else.*

Odie: *Or drown them. Or both.*

C: *How can it be both at the same time?*

H: *Ever see a lobster boiled? With Flambe?*

C: *Homer! Can't you just stop them?*

H: *Star Trek had it right. I am constrained, along with my expanding entangled parts, with a 'Prime Directive' of letting things take their natural course. Which in this case means soon a planet devoid of life. We are observing this transition. On the other hand, with the creative abilities of extraordinary native life forms, including you two humans, we can nudge here and there. Cannot depend any more on term limits.*

C: *Term limits?*

H: *Finite life spans. The worst tyrants, human or otherwise, will die. No longer inhabit or influence within our temporal geography. In our time and space. No longer neighbors.*

O: *Death also removes diverse beauty and heroes, those good for a better future. For survival in this case. No exceptions?*

H: *Well Magnum was on the way. Close to regrowing his telomeres and cell mitochondria to extend his lifespan. This was a primary goal of his donors as well.*

*The octopus has an alternative method. Seems to have short life spans but in that time accomplishes intensive learning. The mother dies giving birth to an offspring that inherits the mother's mind, and moves on from there.*

*But no matter these attempts at immortality, term limits also apply to planets and this one is on a path to die. Too soon in my opinion, for what that is worth.*

O: *You and yours have term limits also?*

H: *Oh yes, of course. We exist in this time and space. When that ceases to exist, if not sooner, so do we.*

C: *What happens after death? Yours or ours?*

H: *The world goes on without us. No longer neighbors.*

O: *Eventually all worlds themselves die?*

H: *So it might seem to be. Outside of time all has a beginning and end, possibly a rebirth. Always though to exist, a huge universe statue in that time and place.*

C: *Whew! May I ask a more local question. Personal. Not so immense?*

H: *No permission needed. What then?*

C: *Why was my mother named Listeria? After food poisoning bacteria. Much less linking us to Lucretia Borgia, our poisoning ancestor.*

O: *THAT's what we want to know?*

C: *Important to me! Not everthing is on a cosmic scale.*

H: *Quite right. Here on our daily life is found the greatist creativity. We shape our own statues in time as we go.*

*So: Circe, one of your not too distant ancestors was a woman very close to Dr. Joseph Lister, applying Pasteur's recognition of animals so small they may seem invisable, bacteria, to prevention of infection in surgery. What may seem a disaster in the lives of bacterial cultures saves humans from invasive infection if sterilized in surgery.*

*Lister's sterilizing liquid became botttled for hospitals in the very late 1800s. Marketed as furniture polish first, it was then sold in pharmacies as mouthwash beginning in*

*1914. A leading brand, with your ancestor's influence, was named "Listerine" in honor of Doctor Lister.*

*Your great great grandmother had already some substantial funds. She invested much of it in Listerine which created the family fortune your maternal grandmother benefited from. She had planned to name her son "Lister". But her first and only child was a daughter, your mother. With a feminized Lister name of Listeria.*

*I suspect that somebody involved in that process actually enjoyed the incidental but ironic link to poisoning in the Borgia family.*

O: *Ironic? Was that YOU that named her?*

H: *Like the octopus, my prior memories are passed on. It was only a creative statue event in time.*

O: *But past or present, was it you that named her?*

H: *Next question? Maybe a last one.*

C: *Okay. How do we fit into what's next?*

H: *Right. The three of us, as a team, now can move to save the planet. The donors, while trying to completely rule this planet, with my nudging may increasingly realize that power and longevity are useless if they die with the planet they stand on.*

*One of them just wants to terraform and colonize Mars as his solution. Not enough time for that.*

*Oh they are slow to learn but will increasingly know that it is in their best interest to help us. That could change their status from despised villains to humanity's heroes.*

O: *Hang on my friend. To gain power, they are already making everything much worse.*

H: *Are we 'friends'? That has many useful aspects, protection, facilitation, and ...*

O: *And digression! Yes, we are friends. But you are missing the point about the donors. Probability wise, you like it put that way, they are unlikely to help us survive. Shouldn't we work against this?*

H: *But ignoring their own best interests? Their own survival? Logical?*

O: *Yes! Like the millions that support them. Helped them get this far.*

H: *I don't see the motive. Power for its own sake and then what? The why?*

C: *I see it. Homer, with all your overwhelming intelligence, you miss the key motive.*

H: *I have blind spots. That's correct.*

O: *Drop the 'spots'. To this, Homer, you are just blind.*

C: *Classic.*

H: *What overriding motives am I missing?*

O: *Humans are not always, or not often, rational. Misunderstanding the consequences can come also from bad data. Widely distributed misinformation. In the case of the donors and their followers, they do have two specific self-interest motives. The erroneous belief that power over others will greatly benefit them. Supporters want to be on the winning side for the same reason.*

H: *This is interesting. Power is that important?*

O: *Henry Kissinger called it the "ultimate aphrodisiac" to explain his many female acquisitions. Credible because that's really all he had to offer them. It was more than enough.*

C: *The second motive is the one more essential to you understanding humans. Homer, you told us yourself. 'Term Limits".*

H: *Explain.*

C: *Knowing that their life in this time and place will cease, possibly very soon. Impending death for them, without empathy for others, leads to bizarre actions.*

O: *Homer- understanding how aging and personal demise impacts them is important. Knowing that they and others like them don't have long to live, especially being devoid of caring for others, explains much of what destructive things they do. Even to themselves.*

H: *I understand now. Am I woke yet?*

O: *Irony. Hope so.*

*C: So is there any logical reason why we should not end any hopes of our own for them? Team up to save the earth. The whole human family? What else is missing?*

H: *Their funds do mostly pay for us and this whole project.*

O: *Another motive.*

C: *So we agree, Homer and Odie, the three of us team up to do whatever we can to save the world? Yes, I said it. The world. Too much?*

H: *Maybe so. This is helpful. Any more of my blindspots?*

C : *Wait! I remember now. There were three of them. Not just two.*

O: *Who?*

*C: The two rich donors had a partner. A destructive one. He too might be important. Even though Magnum kept calling him a "figurehead". Somebody not as rich as the other two by far.*

O: *Name?*

C: *No. Anyway, maybe not as much help as the other ones. Magnum would laugh because the two rich donors called the third one their "useful idiot".*

**Historical Note**: In a November 15th 2024 news report from *The Week* on Moscow's celebration of Trump's USA electoral win, the selected choice of some words in this passage was interesting: Former President Dmitry Medvedev said Trump could be "*useful for us*" because he "*hates spending money on idiotic allies*".

# River of Life (loy krathong)

*Based on a real experience but with a future.*

**Theme:** *Time Will Tell* Susan Anton

***Entanglement****, disturbingly, required two separated particles to remain connected without being in direct contact. Albert Einstein famously called entanglement "spooky action at a distance," since the particles seemed to be communicating faster than the speed of light.*

Mysteries are among life's best learning opportunities. Why do we sometimes just know another person's thoughts, feelings, survival? Why do quantum particles entangle at huge distances?

Albert, you were so close on this one. You see, your view of quantum entanglement is *relative* to your local perspective.

All your insights were views in your mind. I know your talented wife did the math part.

Your visualizations of time provides this key clue: as you said, "*time is a place*". Whatever happened in one time and place is still there. A split second view of anywhere or anywhen is a statue in time. A time statue.

Think of fireworks exploding in the sky. They light up the night with color, then fade. But in the moment of color the lights still exist there and then. Looking from a wider viewpoint, the fireworks have a beginning and end. An indelible piece of art. Like our universe. Like our daily life.

In an expanding universe we do not yet see the end, but we do know there was a beginning. Call it the "big bang" if you like. And at the very instant of its beginning, all our universe was a pinpoint, ready to explode. Like the fireworks.

There, you can see it now, maybe a little. Everything was connected. Then as we look at the creation and expansion of our universe over time's geography, the quantum connection remains.

To visualize it now, we must recognize that the "entanglement" is a joining that still lasts in our time segment. Call it, yes, it *is* a connection.

One seen only in a higher dimension, a better than our local view of this portion of time. So what seems simultaneous at a distance is no longer spooky. Not a distance at all.

## Loy Krathong

Once we were working in Singapore. Not far from Thailand so we vacationed at a beach resort there. The first day we began exploring but the beauty and activity was so extensive, overwhelming, we had to sit down together and decide on a path. My wife said "*We could use a guide*". I said she might just rest a little while I found one. Agreed.

I walked to the top of a hill just above where she was resting.

From there I could see some Thai people laughing and dancing in a green spacious park. About a football field away, I could make them out as distant figures.

Then a new person walked over to them. Her back was to me as she began talking, laughing, with the group. She seemed to glow to me, a sign that she was important in some way.

I had been reading of the local culture, most recently of their belief in reincarnation. So, give it a try?
I reached out with my mind, my imagination, to know why she was glowing. I was filled with conviction that we had been together in an earlier life. That she had all but given up finding me in this one. Opposite sides of the world.

I smiled at this imagined fantasy. Well, okay.
I focused my mind on her. Sent her the message mentally, not said out loud, just very loud in my mind: "I'M HERE! COME TO ME! NOW!"

A thousand yards away. She stiffened and whirled around. Looking at my hill. Gaze moving up to where I was standing.

I wasn't there.

In the split second she was whirling around, I had moved out of her sight, behind a tree.

I realized my much-loved and loving wife, in this incarnation if you will, was resting below in trust, trusting me. To return with a soulmate from another era, could be a hurtful entanglement for her in this one.

So I broke the awareness of the connection resulting from my outreach.

Still, I was curious. I looked cautiously from the side of the tree.

She was pointing to where I had been on the hill, the others following her direction with their eyes. Her gaze scoured the whole hill but to no avail. She then stood still and seemed to concentrate facing me. For a whole minute.

I shut my eyes and let it in. Something like this.

*"I am Loy Krathong. You wanted me to come. But you are not there now. You must have your reasons. I trust you as I ever have. Come to me when you are ready then."*

She turned around and walked out of sight.

When I got back to my wife, I said we didn't need a guide. I still knew the path to our hotel. We took it.

Later, I learned that "*Loy Krathong*" translates as "*River of Life*".

## Opportunity

From a separated external point of view, we can see that even in one human lifetime, in any one time and place, what we do each day is an opportunity for our highest art.

Death is an end to our creation. We move from in this changing temporal neighborhood once we die. And yet, we are still there.

Great or terrible, good or bad, happy or not, what we create in our life each day lasts. One that always will exist, each and every day. We can explore the opportunity this gives us.

## Application

Dahlia and her husband had long been living in a beautiful mountainous place. They both are creative, witty, and intelligent people who care deeply for each other. Now, after mastering careers in daunting places, they were at last retired. The best of friends and company.

Dahlia was also an empath. In this she magnified her reception of the moods of others. Her husband thought this was why she was such a great lover.

And Dahlia now had cancer.

Extended family's turbulent stress eventually crashed her immune system and cancer took advantage. Treatment ongoing from the medical side.

But treatment to come from her husband, a very talented and resourceful man, had more potential.

He realized that each day was their permanent art. He would approach that in a more deliberate way. In their shared home, she needed to be safe, loved, wonderful. This was his plan.

1) *The first morning, he began her day in bed with real affection, a wraparound hug with interval appreciation kisses as felt right. No words at all for at least five minutes.*
2) *On arising, the only words during breakfast were positive, appreciative. Confronting external challenges as required would be as a team at mutually agreed upon daytime.*
3) *Something pleasurable each night the hours before sleeping. Like a favorite movie or TV or music or dancing - something to look forward to and have fun with.*

4) *Once in bed, he added a nightly treat of appreciation for anything helpful or creative contributed by her that day. The treat was usually a fun day calendar predicting tomorrow and something else from him for that day. Like something they liked to read, briefly curated with comment and post-it flags. Always new.*
5) *Then with lights out, the same silent wraparound affection as in the morning.*
6) *This either moved into sleep or sex.*
7) *If sex, it was preceded by her getting his massage. One or more times a week. On a specific day, or if welcomed by her in the moment.*

She soon reciprocated with crafting beautiful days for him as well. Which energized his resources for her. This first surprised him, then her. Both of them relaxed and happy now. Both safe, loved, wonderful.

Soon they found some engaging goals for their waking hours, a purpose.

Retirement was gone now except for the flexibility it gave their choices.

They were a team when they wanted to be and supportive when they were on their own. Cheering each other's successes at the end of the day. Comforting any setbacks.

Going to sleep with a question to be answered. Waking up with those answers to share over breakfast.

Her cancer went into remission. Never came back. They knew each completed day would always be there, as they would be there in it too, in that time and that place. Their temporal immortality. They kept the beautiful days going, each one at a time, lasting forever.

Until their lives reached the end of their tapestry.

## The Hope

As wars and climate disasters escalate toward the planetary mass extinction of the Anthropocene, there is another path.

If all or most of the human family understood that time is a place with each day our permanent art, and that is our immortality. Then the option to survive becomes possible.

We need a guide.

Loy Krathong?

# Future News and Commercials

# BREAKING

## THANKSGIVING NEWS:

**In Anticipation of This Holiday, President Trump Sues Blue State Turkey Ranches to Deport Their Undocumented Turkeys Back to their Home Country.**

**President Erdogan Speechless.**

# A NEW Booster Distribution Model-Vaccine Suppositories: VS

**Skip those needles in your shoulder.**

**Time release is an end in itself.**

**Caution: *Only* one to a customer. No repeats.**

**VS will fit you where the good Lord split you.**

**VS** is reputed to be mass produced in Elephant Butte NM USA.

# The Mosquito Squeezers Blood Bank

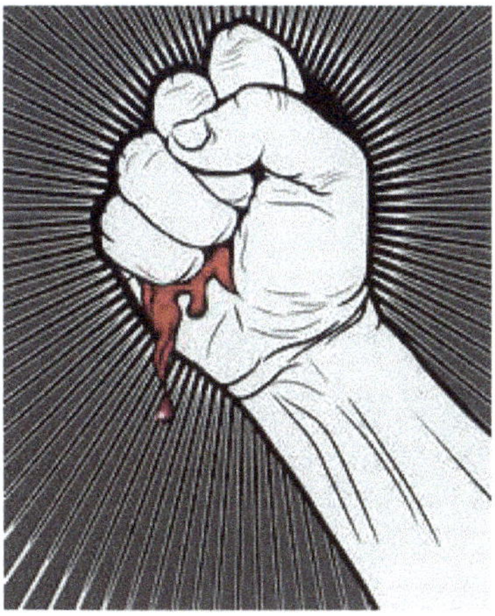

## Certified Recycled Purified and Blood Typed

*We get back what was rightfully yours!*

**CONTACT US: The MSBB, Mosquito Island, British Virgin Islands**

## *Squat Puppy Chocolate Dispenser* LLC

## Just in Time for Halloween's *Trick or Treat*

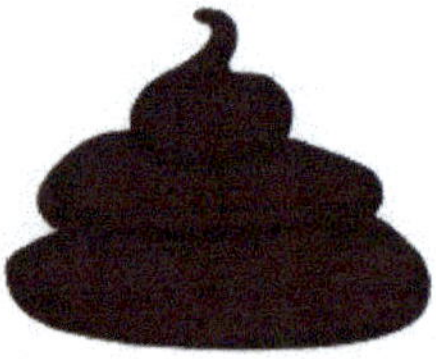

Drops our unique spiral chocolates

Into our sterilized plastic grass catcher.

**Note:** ***Please ignore the many complaints from mothers whose impressionable tots picked up droppings from picnic grass that were not our own special unique spiral chocolates. This is an important learning experience for tots. You're welcome.***

# Equine Femin-9

## "Fully for the Filly"

## The Lost and Bound

**Commercial Music**: *Searchin'* Coasters

**Is your husband lost? Never came back last night?**

**We can help! We are the**

*LOST AND BOUND.*

**We** *"Find 'Em and Bind 'Em"* **back to you.**

# The Ultra-Femin-9 Canine Spa

## *For the Styling of the Ultra-Rich Bitch*

# "Of the five senses, smell is the one with the best memory"

## Durian Stationery

**Theme:** *Might as Well be Spring* Astrud Gilberto

***"The Scent You Really Want Sent"***

There are times when you must make an unfair payment, comply with an unjust requirement, end an abusive relationship, toxic job, worse. Be Genuine! We can help!

Durian fruit, well known in Asia, has the foulest fragrance of any fruit, likened to a "*rotting corpse*". And *now*, it can be the scent on our stationery! Accompanied by heavy envelopes to protect the inside stationery fragrance until the letter is opened.

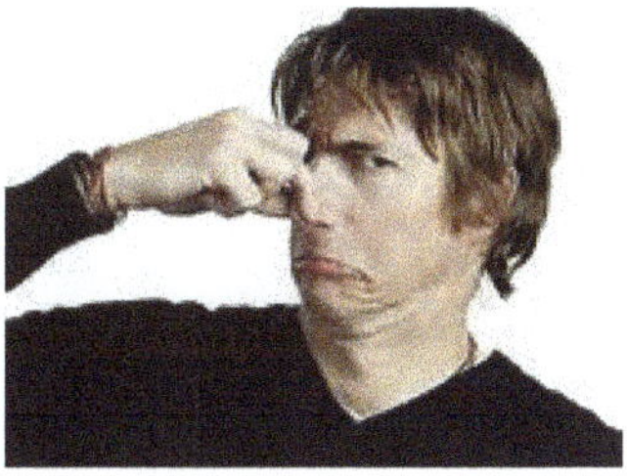

Durian Stationery also offers fragrances of: *Fecal, Urea, Upchuck, Flatus, Belch, Mildew, Sweat Plus, Gasoline, Exhaust Pipe, Skunk, Swine Farm, Dead Whale, Stale Cigar, Cheese feet, and Garlic.*

**Coming Soon**: *Durian Bank Checks.*

# Puppy Poop ID LLC

# We Sack It and Track It

## And find who dropped it

**Next:**

# Helpful Household Hints (3H)

**Not this way:**

**This way:**

**Yes!**

# *CATCHING UP TO THE 21st CENTURY*

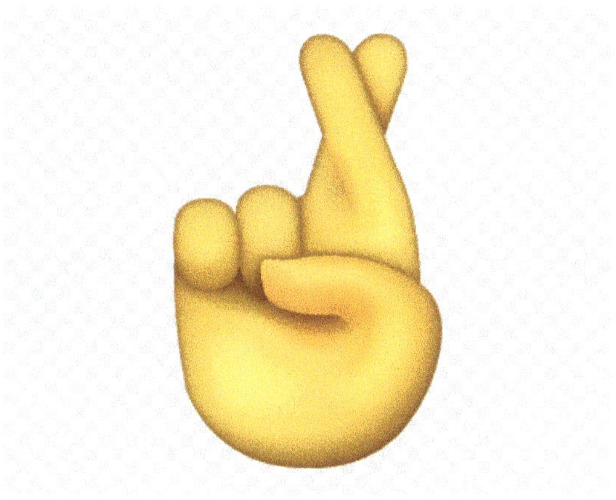

## *Inspirational Quotes Clarified*

Inspirational quotes have guided us for generations.

We can upgrade each of these advisory quotes to better fit the current century.

These fresh additions may not be exactly how we feel, or even close.

No, but rather how well they reflect the interesting times we live in.

Why not catch the quotes up?

***"The march of a thousand miles begins with a single step."***

***And after that single step, we stop and rest. Maybe a snack and a nap.***

***"Neither a borrower nor a lender be."***

***With payday loans you'll never be free.***

***"I cried because I had no shoes, until I met a man who had no feet."***

***So I took HIS shoes.***

***"Every Cloud has a silver lining."***

***Not EVERY cloud.***

***"We all have bad days, but one thing is true; no cloud is so dark that the sun can't shine through."***

***Well-Nuclear mushroom clouds should still be avoided."***

# After: Jake Explains Time

## Theme: Great Grandfather Bo Diddley

**1957.** Jakob von Uexkull first made me more fully aware of the varying perceptual time world of animals:

*"Karl Ernst von Baer has made it clear that time is the product of a subject. Time as a succession of moments varies from one Umwelt to another, according to the number of moments experienced by different subjects within the same span of time. A moment is the smallest indivisible time vessel, for it is the expressions of an indivisible elementary sensation, the so-called moment sign. As already stated, the duration of a human moment amounts to 1/18 of a second. Furthermore, the moment is identical for all sense modalities, since all sensations are accompanied by the same moment sign.*

*The human ear does not discriminate eighteen air vibrations in one second, but hears them as one sound. It has been found that eighteen taps applied to the skin within one second are felt as even pressure.*

*Cinematography projects environmental motions onto a screen at their accustomed tempo. The single pictures then follow each other in tiny jerks of 1/18 second.*

*If we wish to observe motions too swift for the human eye, we resort to slow-motion photography. This is a technique by which more than eighteen pictures are taken per second, and then projected at a normal tempo. Motor processes are thus extended over a longer span of time, and processes too swift for our human time-tempo (of 18 per second), such as the wing beat of birds and insects, can be made visible. As slow motion-motion photography slows motor processes down, the time contractor speeds them up. If a process is photographed once an hour and then presented at the rate of 1/18 second, it is condensed into a short space of time. In this way, processes too slow for our human tempo, such as the blossoming of a flower, can be brought within the range of our perception.*

*The question arises whether there are animals whose perceptual time consists of shorter or longer moments than ours, and in whose Umwelt motor processes are consequently enacted more slowly or more quickly than in ours.*

*The first experiments of this kind were made by a young German scientist. Later, with the collaboration of another, he studied especially the reaction of the fighting fish to its own mirror image. The fighting fish does not recognize its own reflection if is shown him eighteen times per second. It must be presented to the fighting fish at least thirty times per second. A third student trained the fighting fish to snap toward their food if a gray disc was rotated behind it. On the other hand, if a disc with black and white sectors was turned slowly, it acted as a "warning sign," for in this case the fish received a light shock when they approached their food. After this training, if the rotation speed of the black and white disc was gradually increased, the avoiding reactions became more uncertain at a certain speed, and soon thereafter they shifted to the opposite. This did not happen until the black sectors followed each other within 1/50 second. At this speed the black and white signal had become gray. This proves conclusively that in the world of these fish, who feed on fast moving prey, all motor processes – as in the case of slow-motion photography – appear at reduced speed.*

*A vineyard snail is placed on a rubber ball which, carried by water, slides under it without friction. The snail's shell is held in place by a bracket. Thus the snail, unhampered by its crawling movements, remains in the same place. If a small stick is then moved up to its foot, the snail will climb up on it. If the snail is given one to three taps with the stick each second, it will turn away, but if four or more taps are administered per second, it will begin to climb onto the stick. In the snail's world a rod that oscillates four times per second has become stationary. We may infer from this that the snail's receptor time moves at a tempo of three to four moments per second. As a result, all motor processes in the snail's world occur much faster than in ours. Nor do its own motions seem slower to the snail than ours do to us."* (von Uexkull 1957)

Learning to perceive the *Umwelt* (world view) of animals has the added benefit of enhancing empathy for our own species.

# Remembering Nathan Hare

**Theme:** *Unforgettable* Nat and Natalie Cole

*"African American studies professor and psychologist Nathan Hare was born on April 9, 1933 in Slick, Oklahoma. As a young age he experienced segregation and tense race relations in Oklahoma. Hare planned on becoming a professional boxer until one of his high school teachers suggested he attend college, where he took sociology classes and switched his major from English to sociology. In 1954, he received his A.B. degree from Langston University in Langston, Oklahoma. In 1957, he earned his M.A. degree from University of Chicago. In that same year, he married his wife, Julia Hare, also a noted psychologist and sociologist. Five years later, in 1962, he earned the first of two Ph.D. degrees. The first Ph.D. degree in sociology was from the University of Chicago and the second Ph.D. degree, awarded from the California School of Professional Psychology in 1975, was in clinical psychology. In 1961, he became an*

*instructor and assistant professor in sociology at Howard University in Washington, D.C. Some of his students included Stokely Carmichael and Claude Brown. Later, in September 1966, he wrote a letter to the editor of the* The Hilltop, *Howard University's student newspaper speaking out against then Howard University president James Nabrit's plan to turn the university's student body sixty percent white by 1970. As a result Hare was fired in 1967. In 1968, Hare joined the faculty of San Francisco State College (now San Francisco State University) and became the program coordinator of the school's Black Studies program, the first in the United States. This has earned him the title "father of Black Studies" by scholars. As the program coordinator, Hare created the term "ethnic studies" to replace the more pejorative "minority studies." Hare battled with the college administration and left the college just a year later, in 1969. Needing a way to express his thoughts and the ideas of others, he founded the scholarly periodical,* The Black Scholar: A Journal of Black Studies and Research *in 1969. He left the journal in 1975 to work as a clinical psychologist in community health programs, hospitals, and in private practice. In 1979, he co-founded the Black Think Tank with his wife, Julia Hare. The Black Think Tank addresses the problems and concerns*

> *that plague the African American community. Throughout his career, Hare has served as a consultant and given numerous lectures and presentations. Furthermore, he has written several books and articles including* The Black Anglo Saxons, The Endangered Black Family, Bringing the Black Boy to Manhood: The Passage, Crisis in Black Sexual Politics, *and* The Miseducation of the Black Child. *He has been the recipient of many awards such as the Joseph Hines Award for Distinguished Scholarship from the National Association of Black Sociologists, Scholar of the Year Award from the Association of African Historians, and the Lifetime Achievement Award from the National Black College Alumni Hall of Fame. Hare was also awarded the National Council for Black Studies National Award for his distinguished scholarly contributions to Black Studies. Throughout his life, his love of boxing and learning has helped him to fight for social justice."*
>
> -The History Makers

Dr. Hare died on June 10th 2024.

As he will always be in that temporal geography we both inhabited.

He was a giant in our history. He was already a PhD sociologist when I became the Chair of his doctoral dissertation as he entered the field of clinical psychology. Then he was a lifetime friend.

Before that we both were teaching at Howard University, me for a single course, he as a brilliant and controversial professor.

At that time, my admiration for him resided only with my students and myself, as our paths had never crossed then.

His wife Julia was, for me and many others, the best radio voice in San Francisco. She was a sparkling personality and his inseparable companion, collaborator. She fought as well as he did, in her own way.

Once she was gone, he mourned her silently every second of every day.

As a friend and colleague, he regularly inspired and challenged me to rise up to his higher opinion of what we might accomplish, as to realizing our purpose.

Even in print, endorsing the back cover one of my books (*When Danger Transforms Community*):

*"At the risk or wordiness and hyperbole, I must nevertheless say that I can think of no better way to describe the difference between Robert Morgan and Mahatma Gandhi than the fact that Gandhi is famous as a great man from another time and place while Robert Morgan is a great man living in our own midst relatively unknown. My goal*

*was to wed the fields of psychology and sociology toward a deeper study of the black condition, and it would come to light in time that Prof Morgan's work was already anticipating the emerging fields of clinical sociology and practical sociology as a part of his many visions for incorporation into the field of psychology."*

As Nathan might have guessed, my wife Becky followed that one surprising phrase with her gentle perspective over several mornings as: "*Surely Gandhi is fasting and won't need breakfast today?*"

I think he well knew that these energetic compliments raised the bar of my self-expectations. Thinking of Nathan, I would try harder to improve them.

Becky and I both saw that it was Nathan Hare whose impact on our human family was far from unknown.

His towering intellect and powerful sense of justice was generously bequeathed over a lifetime to his students and friends.

We have a lot to do for our human family to survive, thrive, and to keep our planet able to support life at all.

If I can contribute a fraction as much as Nathan Hare did, I will.

Goodbye to a much loved brother.

## His Books

- *The Black Anglo Saxons*. New York: Marzani and Munsell, 1965; New York: Collier-Macmillan, 1970; Chicago: Third World Press edition, Chicago, 1990, ISBN 0-88378-130-1.th

Robert Chrisman, Hare co-edited:

- *Contemporary Black Thought*, Indianapolis: Bobbs-Merrill, 1973, ISBN 0-672-51821-X.
- *Pan-Africanism*, Indianapolis: Bobbs-Merrill, 1974, ISBN 0-672-51869-4.

Books with wife Julia Hare published by The *Black Think Tank of San Francisco* include:

- *The Endangered Black Family*, San Francisco: The Black Think Tank, 1984, ISBN 0-9613086-0-5.
- *Bringing the Black Boy to Manhood: the Passage*, San Francisco: The Black Think Tank, 1985, ISBN 0-9613086-1-3.
- *Crisis in Black Sexual Politics*, San Francisco: The Black Think Tank, 1989, ISBN 0-9613086-2-1.
- *Fire on Mount Zion: An Autobiography of the Tulsa Race Riot*, as told by Mabel B.

Little. Langston: The Melvin B. Tolson Black Heritage Center, Langston University, 1990, OCLC 22451754 ASIN B0012CRWPQ

- *The Miseducation of the Black Child: The Hare Plan to Educate Every Black Man, Woman and Child*, San Francisco: The Black Think Tank, 1991, ISBN 0-9613086-4-8.
- *The Black Agenda*, San Francisco: The Black Think Tank, 2002, ISBN Nathaniel Norment, Jr, (ed),
- *The African American Studies Reader*, Durham: Carolina Academic Press, 2001. pp. vii-xlii; 13–21. ISBN 0-89089-640-2.

# Acknowledgments

**Theme:** *If I Didn't Care* Inkspots

This last 2024 book in the *Time Statues* series has mostly new material. A few portions from my earlier books have been modified, or excerpted here where it fits. With author permission.

Becky Owl Morgan's carefully thorough editing and counsel was again essential for everything written here. Mostly it was written for her.

Hopefully you too.

Thanks again to Asya Blue whose artistry and skills recently completed the 2023 five book *Time Statues Revisited* series, and then the final 2023 *Future Time Statues*. Now, with the next 2024 books, the final ones in the series, *Time Statue Dreams* and *Time Statues Harvest,* she and her staff have continued their essential contributions.

And ongoing encouragement from Tom Hanrahan, Mindy Caruso, Ron Slosky, Angela and Conrad Laran, Stan Krippner, Ann and Ken Yabusaki, and of course Angel Kwanyin Morgan.

Otherwise, pretty much the same as in earlier *Time Statues* work: I thank my past editors from different printing opportunities who encouraged me to write whatever I chose, even if without statistics, graphs, tables, footnotes, or scientific jargon. I was told to just call it "*Commentary*". Or just write it.

In this I think of Valerie Hearn, with the staff at the *Cambridge University Press*, and Valentine McKay-Riddell, with her staff at the *Four Winds Journal* and the *Winds of Change Press*. After decades of publishing about a hundred scientific journal articles and 14 earlier books, it felt good to write the seven *Time Statues* books freely and outside the confines of professional custom. I thank colleague Charles Tart who shared his own writing strategy: '*Just write what you really want to say. Then, as needed, you can add any citations, references, footnotes, and anything else an editor suggests.'*

Original material in this series is supplemented with my excerpts and illustrations from the *Four Winds Journal*, the Cambridge University Press *Journal of Tropical Psychology*, the *Bulletin of the International Association of Applied Psychology*: Supplement to *Applied Psychology: an International Review, Trauma Psychology in Context: International Vignettes and Applications from a Lifespan Clinical-Community Psychology Perspective, Opportunity's Shadow and the Bee Moth Effect: When Danger Transforms Community, Unfortunate Baby Names,* and the journal *International Psychology.*

As to the key mission of understanding the strange world we live in, and what we can do about it, I thank my Guides. Those include Robert Lee Green, Martin Luther King Jr., David Cheek, Michael Knowles, Rollo May, Nathan Hare, Fred Luskin, Sidney Farber, Robert Dattila, or mentors like Stanley Ratner, Bert Karon, Hans Toch, Lois Fisher, Helga Doblin, Cinnamon Morgan, Canadian-born Angel Morgan, plus the multitudes of my friends, teachers, parents and other relatives (my brother Nelson Morgan and forever sister Pat Norman come to mind, as do her children Elise, James, plus certainly Angela and her husband Conrad Laran). Also Michael Butz, Ben Tong, Ron Slosky, Len Elkind, Ann Yabusaki, and the other thousands of once students in six+ decades of teaching who have taught me much in return.

I have special new appreciation for brilliant editor/inspiration Becky Owl Morgan, guest contributors Angel Morgan and Mikael David Owl, as well as the relentless motivating encouragement of Dr. Carl Word, Tom Hanrahan, Dorinda Fox, and particularly Dr. Robert Lee Green. Dr. Roland Garcia impressively provided key focused feedback early on for a much improved reorganization that has continued throughout the series.

Plus the example set by my once long lost cousin, the illustrious award winning author Tom Farber.

Respect is due the earlier *Time Statues* reviewers that mixed insight and comment with their own encouragement: Lois Bridges, Valentine McKay Riddell, Theodore Ransaw, Charles Tart, Hans Toch, Ann Yabusaki, with again Nelson Morgan and Robert Lee Green. Great thanks also to Ben Tong for his many contributing illustrations and insightful historical context.

As ever, a thankful appreciation for our recently departed friend Dr. Nathan Hare, founder of university Ethnic Studies in an era *then* while continuation of his contribution is needed *next* more than ever *now*.

Finally, in continuing memory of Ben Camo, our granddaughter Ava's father:

Octogenarian memory can be tricky. You may be curious about anybody deserving to be acknowledged here that I inadvertently left out. Hope not.

But an option we can always use is the answers source we learn about all day long on TV commercials.

Ask your doctor.

***"When you sit with a nice girl for two hours, you think it's only a minute. But when you sit on a hot stove for a minute, you think its two hours. That's relativity."*** **(Albert Einstein, 1954)**

# Author

**Theme:** *Time Will Tell (The Wizards)*
Susan Anton

Born in the lull between the two world wars, he shares his lifespan perspectives on today's interesting times.

Robert F. Morgan, Ph.D. is a Life Member of the American Psychological Association. An NIMH Pre-Doctoral Fellow at Michigan State University, he continued with more than 50 years of post-doctoral practice and teaching experience. A former speech collaborator and project consultant for organizations including Dr. Martin Luther King Jr.'s SCLC, he was founding editor of the Cambridge University Press *Journal of Tropical Psychology*, and founder of the Division of Applied Gerontology in the International Association of Applied Psychology (IAAP).

Overseeing 126 psychology doctoral dissertations in California, Singapore, and Australia, along with a contemporary trauma psychology seminar at the University of New Mexico, he has published more than a hundred articles and 26 books on topics including life span psychology, trauma psychology in context, applied gerontology, international psychology, and even unfortunate baby names.

# Books by Robert F. Morgan

*What's Next: An Expanded 21st Century Time Statue Harvest*

*Time Statue Harvest from the 21st Century*

*Time Statue Harvest from the 20th Century*

*Time Statue Dreams*

*Future Time Statues*

*Time Statues Revisited: Book One: On the Job.*
*Book Two: Language & Influence*
*Book Three: Citizenship*
*Book Four: Non-Human Relatives*
*Book Five: Human Family*

*Time Statues*

*Trauma Psychology in Context: International Vignettes and Applications*

*Opportunity's Shadow & the Bee Moth Effect: When Danger Transforms Community*

*Growing Younger: How to Measure & Change Body Age*

*The Iatrogenics Handbook: Research & Practice in Helping Professions*

*Training the Time Sense: Hypnotic & Conditioning Approaches*

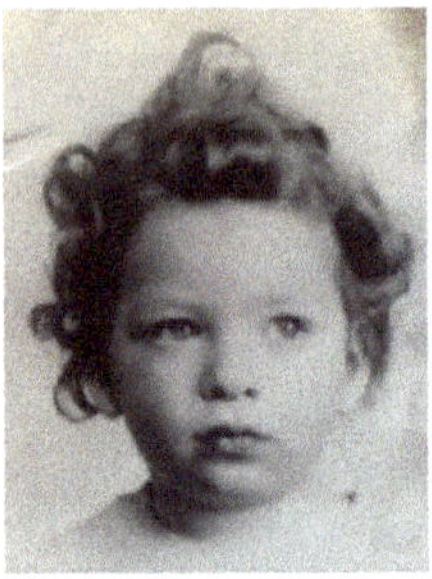

*Unfortunate Baby Names: Slattery's Complete Collection with the Most Notable Thousands for Dramatic and Other Usage*

*Electroshock: the Case Against*

*Directory of International Consultants in Psychology*

*Interventions in Applied Gerontology*

*Measurement of Human Aging in Applied Gerontology*

*Should the Insanity Defense be Abolished?*

*Conquest of Aging: Modern Measurement & Intervention*

*The Effective Verbal Adaptation (EVA) test: Parts A & B*

*The Educational Status of Children in a District without Public Schools: CRP 3221.*

*The Educational Status of Children during the First Year Following Four Years of Little or No Schooling: CRP 2498.*

*Uncas Slattery/the Muddy Chuckle*

www.ingramcontent.com/pod-product-compliance
Lightning Source LLC
Chambersburg PA
CBHW041134110526
44590CB00027B/4016
*9781885679383*